Lighting Design for Modern Houses of Worship

by Richard Cadena

Lighting Design for Modern Houses of Worship

First published March 2008
by Timeless Communications
6000 South Eastern Ave. Suite 14-J
Las Vegas, NV 89119
www.plsnbookshelf.com

ISBN: 978-0-9798107-1-8

ACKNOWLEDGEMENTS

The lighting business is as competitive, if not more so, than any other. In an industry where margins are sometimes as thin as the walls in a cheap hotel, just about every deal is like a chicken bone being fought over by seagulls on the beach. Still, this industry is not like your everyday dime store merchandise. It's different. And it's the people who make up the industry that make it so. The same people who are battling over an account one minute might be socializing and fraternizing the next. And though we might aggressively defend our accounts, it's not uncommon to help other people in the industry, to offer instruction or advice, or to do whatever we can to help another person advance their career.

After more than twenty years in the industry, I've had more than my share of blessings as the recipient of the kindness of the industry. The many people who have helped me are far too numerous to list, but I gratefully acknowledge each and every one. I hope you know who you are! Still, I would be amiss if I didn't acknowledge the contributions of a select few.

Several years ago, I showed Mark Sepulveda a 3D WYSIWYG lighting model on my laptop, and that eventually led to a long relationship and a strong friendship. It also opened the door to personal and professional relationship with all the very fine people at Maxx Technology in Franklin, Tennessee. Most of the work that enabled me to write this book was a direct result of these relationships. I'd like to thank Mark, and everyone at Maxx Technology, including Jay Hall, David King, Neal Watson, Josh Berry, Martin Culpepper, Andrew Wakeman, Paul Duryee, and everyone else at the organization. It has been wonderful to work with you all.

I would also like to thank my publisher Terry Lowe for his support and tolerance of all my extra curricular activities. You're the real brains of the operation, I'm just the "pretty face," but I'm okay with that. (This would be where I would put one of those winking emoticons if this were an e-mail.)

Thank you to my loving wife and daughter, Lisa and Joey Cadena, who always support me in all of my endeavors. (Joey, go clean up your room; love, dad.)

Last, but by no means least, I would like to thank the Lord for all of the guidance and direction in my life.

CONTENTS

CHAPTER 5

CHAPTER 6

CHAPTER 7

YAMAHA

INTRODUCTION

"Art strives for form and hopes for beauty."
— Rose Elizabeth Bird

In some ways, today's lighting systems are like the layers of an onion. The outermost layer reveals only the beauty of the visual art of lighting; the toning and color, the defining shapes and shadows, the complex textures, and the graceful ballet-like movements and crossfades. But if we peel away the first layer we will find another layer with a great deal of work and preparation that went into making it look aesthetically pleasing. The right types and numbers fixtures must first be selected and rigged in the proper place, the lighting angles must be just so, the colors and tones must be chosen, and the intensity levels must be set just right. And if we peel away yet another layer of the onion we will find all of the technology behind the system; the computers, high-tech plastics, optical thin-film coatings, compact arc lamps, robotics, networking, and electronics. But like an onion, the heart of every lighting system, and its most important ingredient of all, is its purpose for being. It's the driving force and the motivation for creating and using the lighting system in the first place.

The lighting designer who designs for a house of worship is in a very special place. That place resides at the intersection of worship, theatre, concert production, and broadcast. To navigate the terrain requires careful deference and respect for the traditions, practices, and desires of the community while exhibiting a solid command of the techniques and skills associated with all of these disciplines. It's challenging, and the accelerating pace of technology doesn't make it any easier.

Rapidly advancing technologies are creating opportunities to refine our production values and offer new ways to approach old problems. Incandescent lamps, for example, have been around for about 120 years and the lamps we use in the vast majority of the ellipsoidal reflector spotlights use virtually the same technology that Edison and Swan invented at the turn of the twentieth century. But new technology is threatening to take its place alongside our tried and true conventional lighting technology. LEDs, compact fluorescent lamps, electroluminescence, and high efficiency incandescent lamps may soon be as commonplace in theatrical lighting as the ellipsoidal is today.

And lamp technology is just the tip of the proverbial iceberg. Not only are we using new technologies in production today, some of which was scarcely heard of 10 or 15 years ago, but we've practically been invaded by media servers, low-res video displays, networking, wireless technology, battery-powered this and Internet-enabled that. No sooner do we familiarize ourselves with one rev of software before the next rev is thrust upon us.

The good news is that there is hope for those of us who are willing to put forth the effort, and it's not as difficult as we might think. The key is to understand the fundamentals underlying the technology. To the initiated, any new technology is but a manifestation of an existing principle in a unique presentation. LEDs are another light source, albeit one with different characteristics than an incandescent lamp. But they follow the same principles, just as do compact fluorescent lamps, electroluminescent sources, and any other emerging technology.

The purpose of this book is to provide a solid foundation of fundamentals that apply in any given situation and that will adapt to any new technology. It is a guide to the future of designing with light.

Today's lighting designer does indeed face many challenges, but the designer working in a place of worship has the advantage of working for a higher purpose. And that, along with a grasp of the fundamentals, will get us over the hurdles of technology and the challenges of designing with today's lighting systems.

Chapter 1

GOALS, OBJECTIVES, METRICS AND METHODS

"Your purpose explains
what you are doing with your life.
Your vision explains
how you are living your purpose.
Your goals enable you
to realize your vision."
— Bob Proctor

GOALS, OBJECTIVES, METRICS AND METHODS

We live in an ever increasing visually stimulating environment. A vast number of images and messages vie for our attention in an increasing number of mediums. We are constantly bombarded with aural and visual messages from television, cell phones, billboards, newspapers, magazines, the Internet, and even T-shirts and sneakers. To divert and hold another person's attention today is no easy task.

For the lighting designer in a house of worship, the objectives are easy definable: focus and hold attention; provide enough illumination for the congregation (both for the young and the elderly) and possibly for video; and make it aesthetically pleasing without creating a distraction from the message. But to implement these objectives is not always as easy as it may seem. There are typically those contentious issues like budget and committee approvals that have to be addressed even before a lighting design is drawn up. Then there is the little matter of "design" that must first be understood and then carried out.

Fortunately, much of lighting design is objective and measurable. Illumination levels, uniformity of light levels across a specified area, color temperature (the balance between red and blue in the spectrum of white light), and color rendering are all examples of concrete measures of lighting quantity and quality. These are hard and fast objectives that we can work toward using established methods, known relationships, and a little calculation. If we get it right then we can manipulate the visual environment in order to achieve our goals and objectives.

On the other hand, there is another side of lighting design that is more subjective and perhaps a little more challenging to define. What "looks good" is a matter of opinion, and perhaps even more elusive is the question of how to manipulate our lighting tools to create a "desirable" or "pleasing" look. There are a variety of ways to change the look and feel of a scene – using color, diffusion, interference medium (fog or haze), lighting levels, lighting angles, etc. These are all tools and techniques that we use to sculpt the visual environment.

When it comes to creating a visual environment in a place of worship, the lighting designer is typically subordinate to a higher purpose. Our job as a lighting designer is to create the right visual environment to support the higher purpose without eclipsing it. The effective lighting designer is one who can use the available tools to the best advantage within the scope of purpose. It is a unique application using many of the same tools as other lighting disciplines. With some knowledge, some practice and a little experience, we can be an effective lighting designer who works to serve the higher purpose.

WHAT IS LIGHTING DESIGN?

Lighting design is the process of using light to shape the visual environment in order to achieve a stated objective or set of objectives. The objectives can range from the subjective, such as "livening up" a room, to the more concrete, such as increasing visibility for the elderly. A lighting designer typically has a range of tools from which to choose, and understanding how those tools work and how best to apply them to a specific situation is a designer's stock in trade. Lighting design is not an exact science; rather it is a mix of the subjective and the objective. If you asked 10 different lighting designers the best way to approach a lighting project you're likely to get 10 different solutions. There is no one right or wrong way to do it. There are many different approaches that are equally valid and might yield equally good results. The final criteria are the achievement of your stated objectives and a good (or great) final result. That's why it's important to define our goals and objectives before approaching a solution to the design.

Lighting design can be learned and with practice it can be honed and improved upon. Once we understand the basics, then more research, experience, experimentation, and exchanging ideas with other lighting designers will be our best teachers. The more we work with lighting the more techniques we will develop and the more we will train our eyes and sharpen our skills.
One way to train your eye for lighting is to look out the window when you're flying at night. When you are on your final approach and you are close to the ground, there are lots of lighting "canvasses" to see and observe. For example, you can compare and contrast the color temperature, intensity, and uniformity of the lighting in sports arenas, parking lots, and city streets. After you land, it's fun to drive to one of your targets and observe the same spot from the ground.

There is much to know about lighting and lighting design, and with the rapid pace of technological change, there is more to know every day. But as long as we understand the fundamentals then we can more easily deal with changing technology and changing products. Once we understand the characteristics of light then it doesn't matter what the light source is; it can be incandescent, fluorescent, discharge, LED or anything else, and the fundamental principles such as the "quality" of light still apply. The key is to have a firm grasp of the basic concepts.

Concepts:

- Lighting design is the process of using light to shape the visual environment in order to achieve a stated objective or set of objectives.
- Color temperature is the balance between the red and blue content in white light. It is measured in Kelvins; incandescent lamps have a color temperature of 3200K and daylight has a color temperature of about 5600K.

Words to know:

- Color temperature

Design goals can be defined in terms of **visibility**, **contrast**, **uniformity**, **quality of light**, **modeling**, **depth** and **aesthetics**.

BEGINNING A PROJECT: WHAT ARE YOUR DESIGN GOALS?

Abraham Lincoln once said, "Give me six hours to chop down a tree and I will spend the first four sharpening the axe." This advice is not only appropriate for clearing land but it's also very appropriate for lighting design. Before you begin your lighting project, you should bring into sharp focus your goals and objectives. What is it that you are trying to achieve with the lighting system? Is it simply for visibility or is there more to it than that? The design criteria should be tailored to the job at hand. Some of the criteria that you might include in your stated objectives are outlined below.

VISIBILITY

Visibility is one of the most common lighting design goals. If you are lighting a platform with a speaker or other subjects, then the subject(s) should be lit to a certain level of illuminance as measured in lux or footcandles; otherwise it will be difficult to make out facial features and expressions. Our visibility goal should be quantified by the amount of illuminance we are targeting. We will discuss this in detail later on.

If there is image-magnification or video acquisition, then the illuminance requirements will change because a video camera has different lighting requirements than the human eye. You should consult with the video crew to find out their expectations ahead of time.

FOCUSING ATTENTION

Over the course of a typical service, it's natural for people's attention to drift. By keeping the platform and the subjects well lit and keeping the peripheral areas at lower illuminance levels, we can help keep focus attention where it should be. Focusing attention is as much a function of the lighting contrast, that is, the difference in illumination levels between the areas of interest and the areas of less importance, as much as it is a function of overall illuminance levels. If everything in a room is lit to 300 footcandles, the eye has no focal point and there is nothing to draw the eye or compel it to stay focused on the subject. If, on the other hand, the subject is lit to 150 footcandles and the rest of the room is lit to 25 footcandles, then the eye is more likely to stay focused on the well-lit subject rather than wander around a darker room.

VIDEO REQUIREMENTS

Most modern houses of worship today are reinforced with live video, either in the form of image-magnification (I-mag) or "B-roll," which is pre-produced content for playback. If the sanctuary you are lighting has video cameras, then the lighting requirements could change dramatically. The light levels, uniformity, color temperature, and direction of lighting are all subject to critique and debate by the video crew. It's best to communicate early and stay in close communication with them to determine their requirements and expectations. Ask the head of the video department about their expectations for light levels on the platform.

Video and image-magnificaion alters the lighting design criteria.

Modern video cameras require lower light levels but higher lighting levels still produce a better signal-to-noise ratio with a less grainy picture. One of the biggest issues to deal with when video is involved is the uniformity of light across the platform, particularly if the subject likes to move around a lot or if there are many subjects spread across the platform. If the light level varies from one spot to the next then the video engineer will have to "ride the iris" or "shade the cameras" to correct the exposure levels every time the camera moves. When that happens then the lighting crew will usually hear about it.

MODELING OBJECTS

One of the main objectives of lighting design is to give form and definition to the subject. This is commonly accomplished by "modeling" the subject with light. That simply means that you can accentuate the texture and form of an object or a subject by lighting it at certain angles and carefully controlling the intensity of the various lights. Lighting an object only from the front tends to make it look to the human eye as if it is flat. It hides the definition, features and depth of the subject. On the other hand, a video camera tends to accentuate the very shadows that

Lighting can enhance the audience's experience by creating an aesthetic mood with color and projection.

give an object shape and form. To compound the issue, a video camera has the ability to zoom in on the subject and magnify the intensity of shadows. Therefore, we have to distinguish whether we are lighting primarily for the human eye — i.e., the congregation — or whether we're lighting for the camera. If we're lighting for the camera then we might want less modeling and more flat lighting. But if we're lighting primarily for an audience, then we can model the subject so that we can illuminate its distinguishing characteristics and make it look more natural from a distance.

CREATING A SENSE OF DEPTH

Lighting can also create depth and give the appearance of space. By controlling the intensity of light at different areas of the platform, for example, highlighting the downstage area and dimming the upstage area, we can give it spatial reference and definition. That helps keep it from looking as if all of the subjects on the platform are on top of each other. We can also create depth by using backlight to highlight the form and shape of a subject.

Concepts:

- Set design goals before starting a lighting design project.
- Define your goals in terms of visibility, contrast, uniformity, quality of light, modeling, depth and aesthetics.

Words to know:

Lux; footcandles; illuminance; contrast; I-mag; B-roll; signal-to-noise; "ride the iris"; "shade the camera"; modeling; aesthetics

AESTHETICS AND MOOD

By using color, patterns, and projections, we can change the aesthetics and influence the mood of the audience. It can be bright and cheery, dark and moody, or we can simply paint a picture with an interesting aesthetic appeal. Of course, any two people may not necessarily agree on what constitutes an "aesthetically pleasing" look, but there are certain principles to help guide us in this regard. For example, the color blue is most difficult for the human eye to focus, so it tends to obscure features. Yellow is a very bright color. The combination of blue and yellow creates a strong contrast. There are many other principles of colors and color combinations that are very useful as a starting point in lighting and scenic design. We will discuss these in more detail later on.

In a perfect world there would be a very clear delineation between each of our objectives; in the real world there is a lot of gray area. The experienced designer recognizes the conflicts, takes into consideration all of the design criteria, and makes design choices based on a balanced evaluation of the needs of the production. The end result should satisfy all of the competing goals and objectives.

PRAYER

The lighting designer needs to be concerned with a handful of lighting measurements; how much light is produced by a luminaire, how strong the light is in a particular direction, how much light is distributed in a certain area, or how much light is reflected back to the eye or to a camera. Ultimately, the main reason we need to understand these measurements is so that we can use them to decide which lighting instruments to use and to set our goals and objectives. We also need to understand them so that we can measure how well we've met those goals and objectives. The data provided by luminaire manufacturers can be presented in several different formats and we need to be able to decipher it in any form. We should be able to turn the data into useful information about the size and intensity of the beam or field at a given throw distance. Before we start laying out our light plot, we will look at some of the metrics of lighting, specifically the measure of luminous flux, illuminance, luminous intensity, and luminance.

LUMINOUS FLUX

Luminous flux is measured in lumens and it tells us how much light is coming from a lamp or luminaire. Lamp manufacturers often supply data about the total luminous flux for a particular lamp but once it goes in a luminaire, some of the flux is lost to inefficiency. Therefore, we can think of the luminous flux of a luminaire as the total luminous flux of the lamp minus the luminous flux that the fixture is unable to capture and redirect out of the front of the fixture.

ILLUMINANCE

Illuminance is the amount of light falling on a surface in a unit area. It is most often the metric used to design and measure the performance of a lighting system. In the English system illuminance is measured in footcandles (lumens per square foot) and in the metric system it is measured in lux (lumens per square meter). To calculate the illuminance from the luminous flux produced by a luminaire, you can divide the luminous flux by the area over which the light is spread.

Illuminance = luminous flux ÷ area

If the area is given in square meters, then the result will be in lux; if the area is given in square feet, then the result will be in footcandles.Sometimes the area in question has to be calculated based upon the beam angle or field angle of the luminaire. We will discuss this in greater detail later on.

If we think of the luminous flux as a can of paint (the can of paint is the total amount of light produced by the luminaire), then you can think of the illuminance as the thickness (brightness) of the paint applied to a canvass. You can spread it very thinly and cover a large area or you can put on a very thick coat and cover a smaller area. Similarly, concentrating all the light from a fixture in a small area results in higher illuminance and spreading it out in a large area results in lower illuminance. A handheld illuminance meter, such as a Minolta T-10, can be

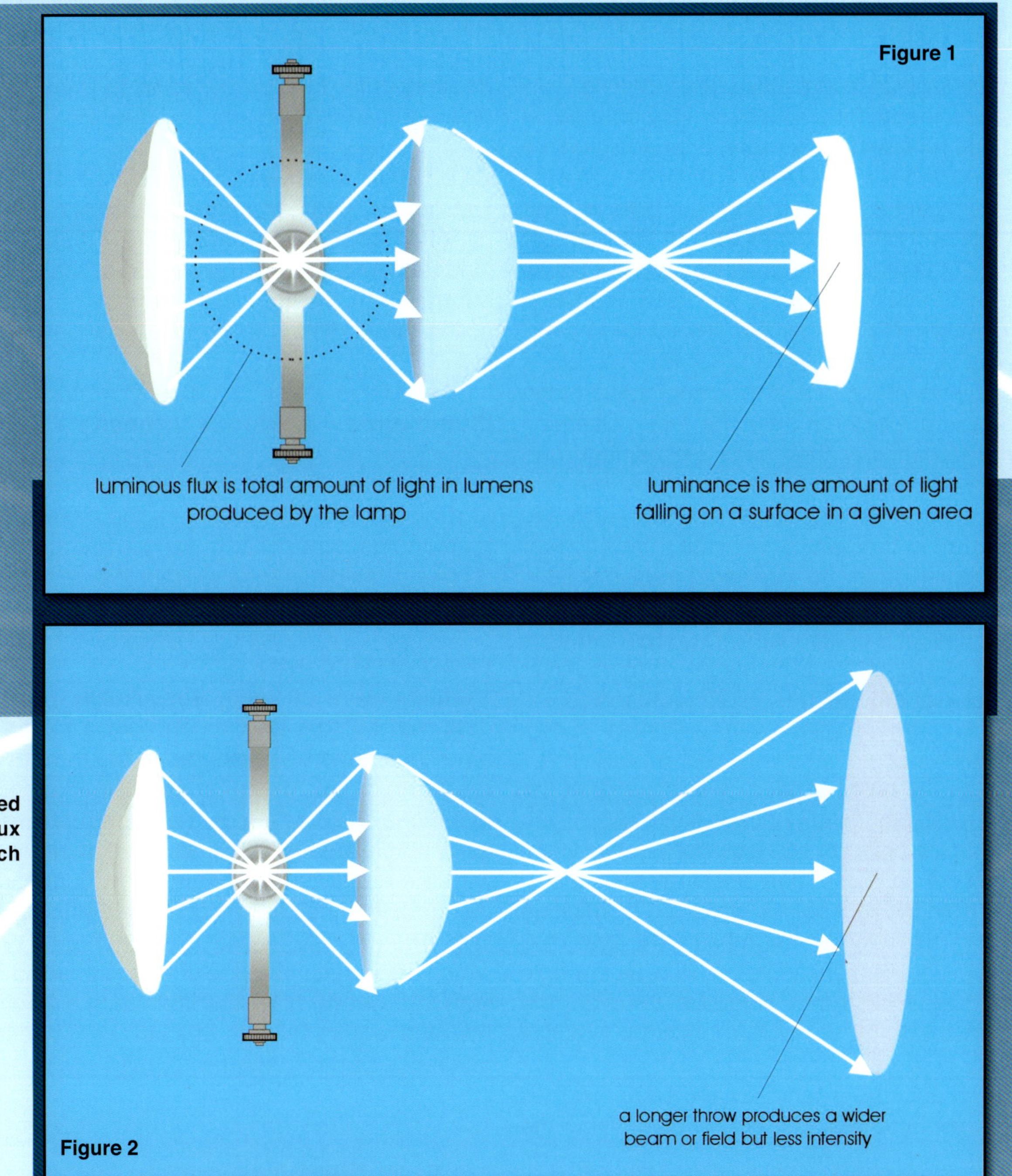

Illuminance is related to the luminous flux and the area in which the light falls.

used to measure the illuminance of a given beam or field.

The illuminance requirements for a sanctuary vary from about 80 footcandles to 150 footcandles or more, depending on the circumstances. The presence or absence of video cameras will influence the illuminance requirements, but bear in mind that as a general rule of thumb, you should light the platform to about twice the illumination level produced by the house lighting in order to preserve the contrast you need and focus attention on the platform. Remember that it's easier to over-design the lighting and use dimmers to lower the light levels to meet the requirements of video and the congregation than it is to add lighting and electrical after the fact. Dimming incandescent lights does lower their color temperature and tones them towards the red end of the spectrum, but that can be easily addressed by adding color correction gels. We should also keep in mind that lamps will lose intensity over time due to lumen depreciation. So we should always build in some overhead to make allowances. For these reasons, it is usually sufficient to design a church lighting system to target an illuminance level of about 150 footcandles or more. Over time, the actual level may drop to 100 to 125 footcandles.

LUMINOUS INTENSITY

Luminous intensity, as the name implies, is a measure of the intensity of light at a given point and in a certain direction. If you stand, for example, on the platform and look directly into a light source, then you can get an idea of how bright the source is. If you then look away from the light source while you're standing in the same spot, the intensity will be much less, assuming you're not looking into another light source. This is an example of gauging the intensity of light in a particular direction. We can quantify that measure by using the luminous intensity yardstick.

Luminous intensity is measured in candelas and it is sometimes used by luminaire manufacturers as a way of quantifying the intensity of the light produced by their instrument. This is very different than the luminous flux metric.

Given the luminous intensity of a particular lighting instrument, you can calculate the illuminance in a certain direction and at a particular throw distance by dividing the luminous intensity by the square of the throw distance. Put another way, the luminous intensity drops off as the square of the throw distance. This is known as the inverse square law.

illuminance = luminous intensity ÷ distance squared

For example, if a luminaire produces 100,000 candelas at a distance of 10 feet, then the illuminance will be 1000 footcandles. Note that if we double the throw distance to 20 feet, the illuminance drops off by a factor of four, to 250 footcandles.

PHOTOMETRIC DATA

Manufacturers of luminaires usually provide photometric data that tells us how much light a fixture produces. This data is sometimes presented in the form of a chart showing the beam or field diameter and illuminance at various throw distances. In some cases the photometric data is presented as a single figure, such as the luminous intensity (along with the beam or field angle). The illuminance at any given distance then has to be calculated using the inverse square law. Alternatively, some manufacturers provide IES files, which are iso-illuminance charts formatted according to the standard set forth by the Illuminating Engineering Society. IES files require the use of a software package designed to make use of the formatted photometric data.

Figure 1

Throw Distance (d)	37.2′ 11.3m	44.7′ 13.6m	52.1′ 15.9m	59.6′ 18.2m
1/10 Peak Diameter	10′ 3.0m	12′ 3.7m	14′ 4.3m	16′ 4.9m
FC	272	188	139	106
Lux	2930	2025	1495	1140

10.5° ½ Peak

15.3° 1/10 Peak

Beam Angle

Field Angle

Typical photometric chart showing throw distance, field width and illuminance.

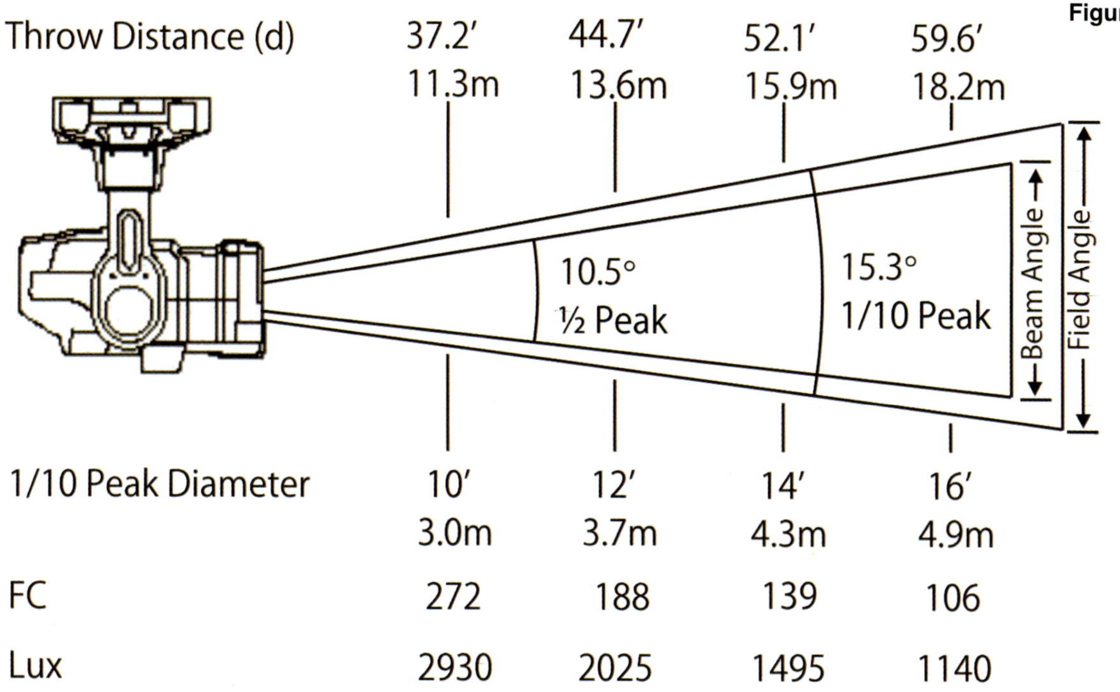

Figure 2

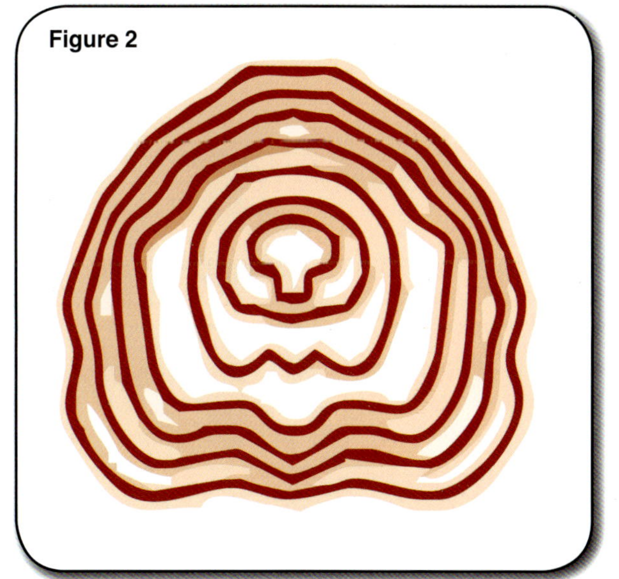

Iso-illuminance chart showing lines of equal illuminance.

LIGHT LEVELS FOR VISIBILITY

If there is no live video reinforcement (as opposed to pre-recorded video playback), then the lighting criteria are different than a service with video cameras. The typical considerations are illuminance, modeling, depth, aesthetics and focus of attention. The uniformity across the platform is less of an issue because the human eye is much more forgiving than a video camera. By the same token, the color temperature (balance between red and blue) and the balance between green and magenta is less of an issue with a live audience. In most cases, 100 to 125 footcandles is sufficient provided the ambient lighting can be controlled. In addition, it's important to use at least three-point lighting (see the McCandless Method below) to model the subject. Layering the lighting to create depth on the platform helps focus and keep attention where it should be. And finally, a bit of color splashed on the set will give the services an aesthetic appeal.

Layering the light helps create depth and separation. In this photo, Mark Schultz is the center of focus while most of his band is underlit to keep them in the background.

LIGHT LEVELS FOR VIDEO

When a service includes live video reinforcement, the lighting design becomes much more critical and demanding, and a number of new design criteria need to be considered. In addition to meeting the minimum illuminance levels, modeling, creating depth and providing aesthetic appeal, the key (front) light should be as uniform as possible across the acting area to avoid hot spots and cold spots on video. The smallest variations in illuminance can produce noticeable problems on the display, even if they are not noticeable with the naked eye. If the acting area is small and the speaker is not a walker, then it's relatively easy to provide uniform front lighting with one or two Lekos or a couple of PAR cans. (Always remember to light the area around a podium as well as the podium in case a guest is called to the front of the stage). But if the acting area is large, then it becomes a bit more challenging to provide uniform lighting across the platform with several fixtures. (We will discuss this more under the topic "4-Point Lighting.")

Modern video cameras are much more sensitive to light than they used to be. Therefore, they can yield very good results with much less illuminance. However, you should be keenly aware of the tradeoffs between capturing video in bright lighting conditions and low light conditions. In bright light, the video engineer shades the camera such that the iris aperture is smaller; in low light the iris is opened more to allow more light to reach the video sensors. The way the background renders on the video monitor is dramatically affected by the size of the iris. A large aperture creates a short depth of field and the background is thrown out of focus. A smaller aperture creates a longer depth of field and the background is rendered in sharp focus.

If you are lighting a subject who is standing at a podium or wandering the platform delivering a message, it is very distracting for the viewer when the church elders or the choir is in sharp focus in the background. It's especially distracting if they are talking, moving, or otherwise drawing attention to themselves when the attention should be focused elsewhere. For that reason, it is often more effective to decrease the illuminance on the platform so that the iris can open more and the background will be a soft blur.

On the other hand, using higher illuminance levels still translates to a higher signal-to-noise ratio on camera. But always defer to the video department because they are the ones who are ultimately responsible for the look on video.

WHITE BALANCE

In addition to uniformity, the video camera should be "white balanced" to the lighting system so that all colors render correctly on the display. If there are both tungsten lamps (color temperature 3200K) and daylight lamps (color temperature 5600K or higher), then one group of them will have to be corrected with gels to match the color temperature of the other group. Some designers prefer to balance the camera to tungsten and correct the discharge lamps while others prefer to balance the camera to daylight and correct the tungsten lamps. Occasionally some lighting designers split the difference and balance everything to 4000K or 4200K. If there is an overwhelming number of one type of lamp versus the other, then your choice may be obvious; go with the color temperature of the dominant source. On the other hand, your design choice might be influenced by the ambient light conditions or by the video crew. If the event is outdoors or near large windows with lots of natural light, then it might be advantageous to balance to daylight. On the other hand, during an indoor event with lots of conventional lights and few discharge lamps it would be easier to balance the lighting to tungsten.

To correct to tungsten, use CTO (correct to orange) filters and to correct to daylight use CTB (correct to blue) filters. Each of these filters is available with varying amounts of correction. One full CTO, for example, will correct a 5600K source to 3200K, while a half CTO will correct daylight to about 4400K. Color correction filters are typically available in 1/8, ¼, ½, ¾, and full values.

GREEN/MAGENTA BALANCE

Sometimes discharge lamps in certain automated lighting fixtures are tinted towards green and away from magenta. It can be caused by the infrared (heat) filter in a fixture or the coating on a dichroic glass reflector. Whatever the cause, it creates problems, particularly for the video crew. It may or may not be obvious to the naked eye but if there is a green balance problem it will show up on video. A vectorscope (an instrument used by video engineers to measure color, both hue and saturation, in a video signal) can be used to objectively determine if there is a color problem and, if so, just how big of a problem it is.

During the setup of the video cameras, a camera is balanced by pointing it to a white card that is illuminated by the key light or video wash. The video engineer monitors the signal produced by the camera and makes adjustments to the camera based on what is seen on the vectorscope. In the picture at the top right, a perfectly balanced camera reading a white card displays a signal at the center of the vectorscope. In the picture on at the bottom right, the signal falls in the area of the green, indicating that the lighting needs to be corrected towards magenta. A minus green filter will address the problem by shifting the color away from the green spectrum and towards the magenta spectrum.

Green is not a flattering color for human skin, so this can be a critical issue, particularly if there is video present in the production.

Figure 1

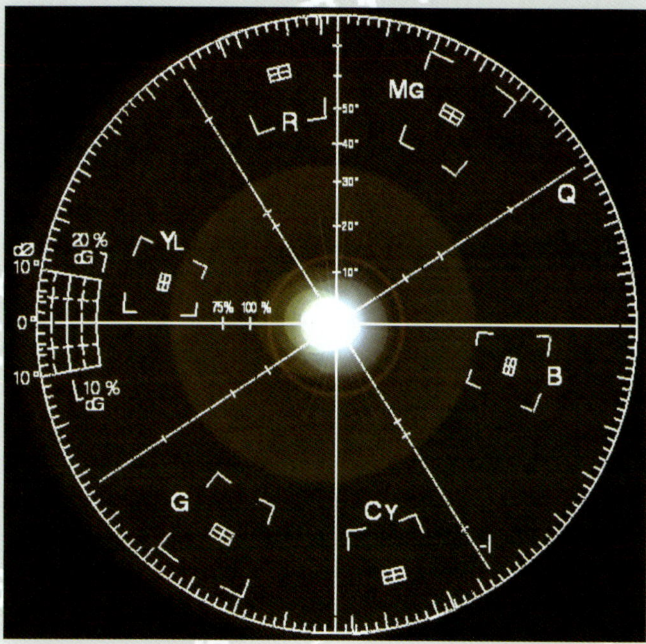

Figure 2

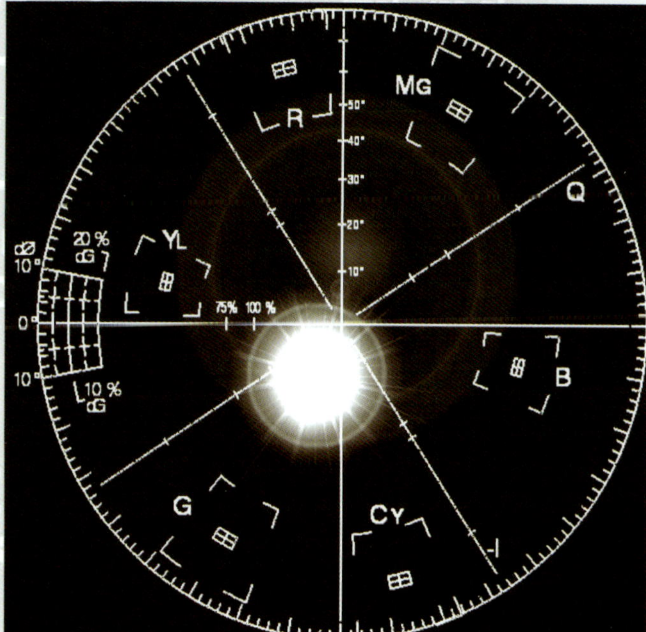

Concepts:

- Illuminance is the amount of light falling on a surface in a unit area as measured in lux (metric system) or footcandles (English system).
- Luminous flux is the total amount of light produced by a lamp or luminaire as measured in lumens.
- Most sanctuaries typically require about 100 to 150 footcandles on the platform, depending on the absence or presence of video acquisition.
- Typical considerations in lighting for visibility include illuminance, modeling, depth, and aesthetics.
- Typical considerations in lighting for video include illuminance, modeling, depth, aesthetics, uniformity, and color balance.
- A vectorscope is used to illustrate the chromaticity of a video signal.

Formulas

Illuminance (footcandles or lux) = luminous flux (lumens) ÷ area (square feet or square meters)

Words to know:

metric; luminous flux; lumens; illuminance meter; live video reinforcement; hot spot; cold spot; Leko; incandescent; discharge lamp; tungsten; daylight; CTO; CTB; vectorscope; minus green filter.

I believe in You, I believe in You
God of Life
I believe in You

THE MECHANICS OF LIGHTING DESIGN

"Even so let your light shine before men;
that they may see your good works,
and glorify your Father who is in heaven."
— Matthew 5:16

Chapter 2

THE MECHANICS OF LIGHTING DESIGN

Lighting design can be dichotomized between that which is objective and measurable and that which is subjective and not strictly measured. The objective, measurable part of lighting design is structured on the application of known relationships to find the optimal number of luminaires and their optimal positions and geometric arrangement to satisfy our design criteria. In this chapter we will discuss the more scientific, calculated side of lighting design with less emphasis on the artistic side. Later on we'll discuss the more subjective and artistic production values. When we put the two together, the result will be a well-designed lighting system that reflects equally the art and the science of lighting design.

Stanley McCandless was a Yale University Department of Drama professor who taught the first lighting design class ever. He was also the first to spell out a methodical way of creating a stage lighting plot. Since he was trained architect, his method is very scientific and straightforward. The McCandless method is still mostly applicable today, except for portions of his book which deal with control and technology. If you understand the McCandless approach to lighting design then you can easily adapt his methods to most lighting situations. Although his first book, "A Method of Lighting the Stage" (1932) is no longer in print, his approach lives on.

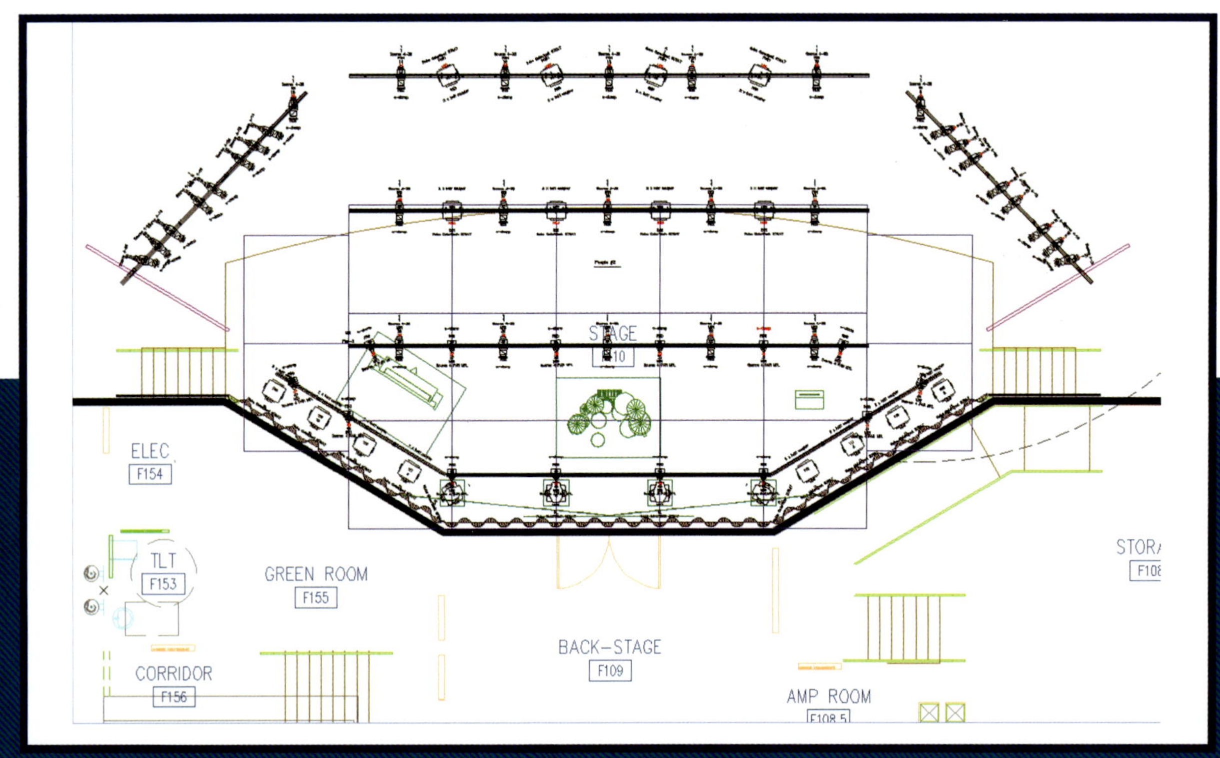

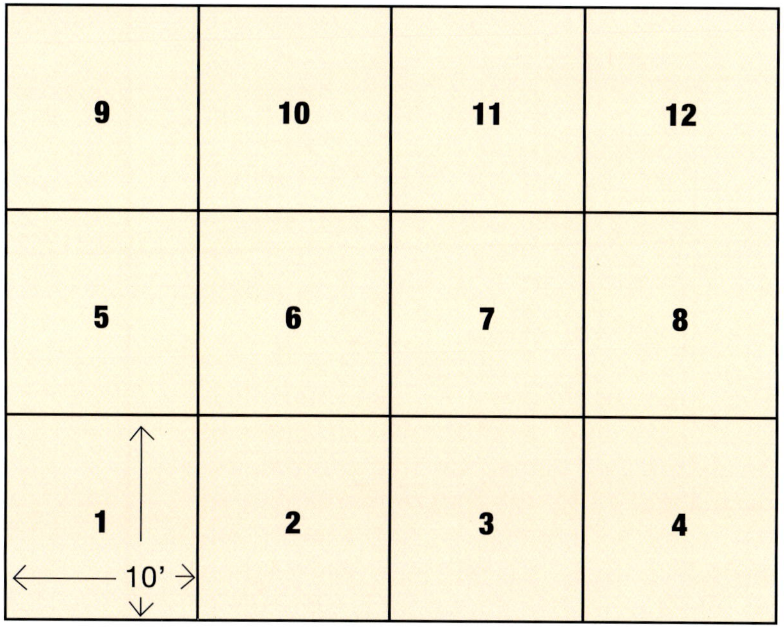

THE MCCANDLESS METHOD

The McCandless method is considered by some people to be outdated today because some of the technology and control methods mentioned are out of date. But the basic principles still apply because the physics and science never change. It's a very good starting point for learning about lighting design and illuminating a subject and a set. By making a few changes, we can adapt it to many situations.

The McCandless method involves dividing a stage into "acting" areas, lighting each area with two lights, then toning and blending, lighting the background and creating special effects. The first step is to mark our acting areas by dividing the platform into eight to 10 feet squares as shown in the diagram above. The exact size of the acting areas depends on the size of the platform. Choose a size that is evenly divisible. For example, a 50'-wide platform can easily be divided into five 10' acting areas while a 48'-wide platform is more easily divided into six 8' acting areas.

9	10	11	12
5	6	7	8
1 (10')	2	3	4

If we are working with a CAD drawing, we will create a new layer and call it "grid" or something equally descriptive. We will place one 10'x10' square in the downstage center location at the podium or where the pastor will be located most of the time. We then create a matrix of squares every 10 feet and cover the entire platform with adjacent 10-foot square areas. Each area represents an individual area to be lit with front light, side light, and back light. This will give us the flexibility to light one section or the entire platform. Choosing the lights, where to locate them, and how to use them is the subject of the balance of this chapter.

KEY AND FILL LIGHT
Once we have created a grid, we will light each acting area with two lights from different angles in order to model the subject. We'll talk about where to locate the two lights shortly.

The type of fixtures to use and their illuminance at a given throw distance can be determined based on the photometric data supplied by the fixture manufacturer. We need to choose a fixture with the correct luminous flux and lens combination so that it produces the target luminance at a throw distance that will work for us. We will want each light to fill one acting area, so we need a beam width of about ten feet. That will give us enough coverage for one acting area with some spill to overlap with the adjacent area. (More on that later.)

Once we sort through our options and find the right instrument, then we can begin laying them into our light plot. The lights should be positioned so that they are 45 degrees above an imaginary horizontal plane from the subject and 45 degrees to either side of a vertical plane bisecting the subject. (See illustrations) One of them will

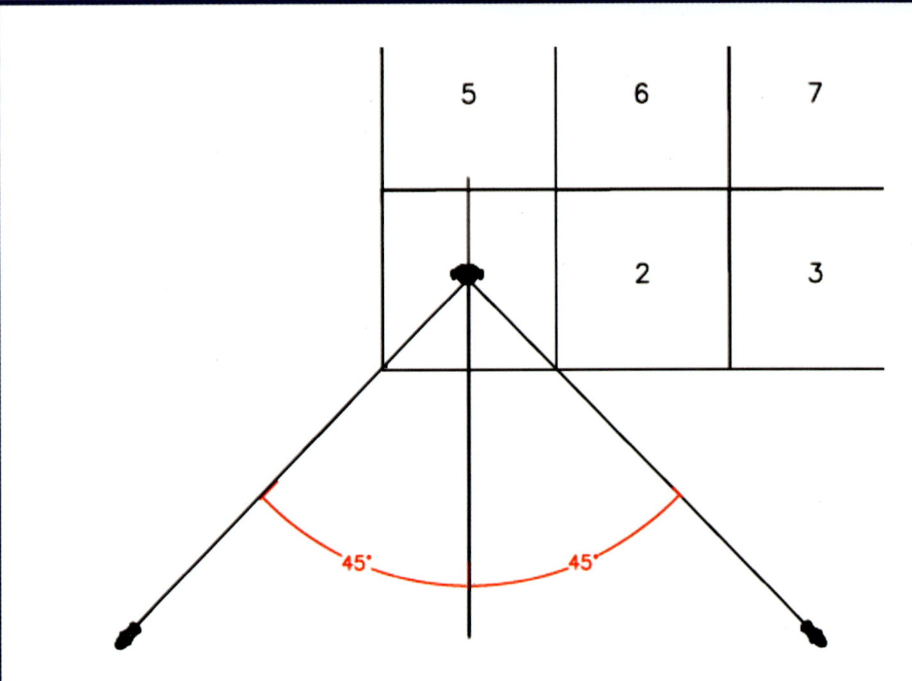

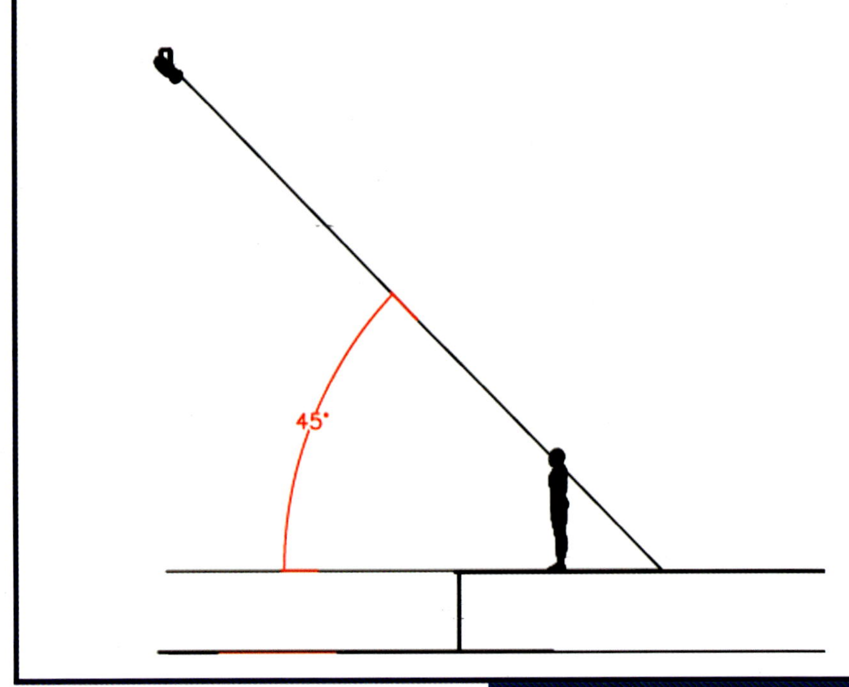

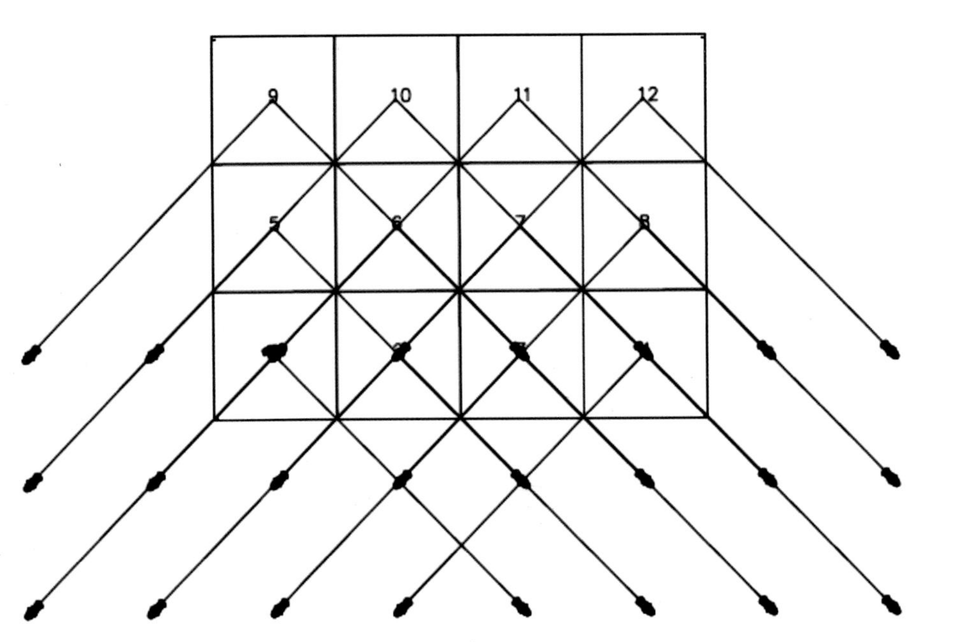

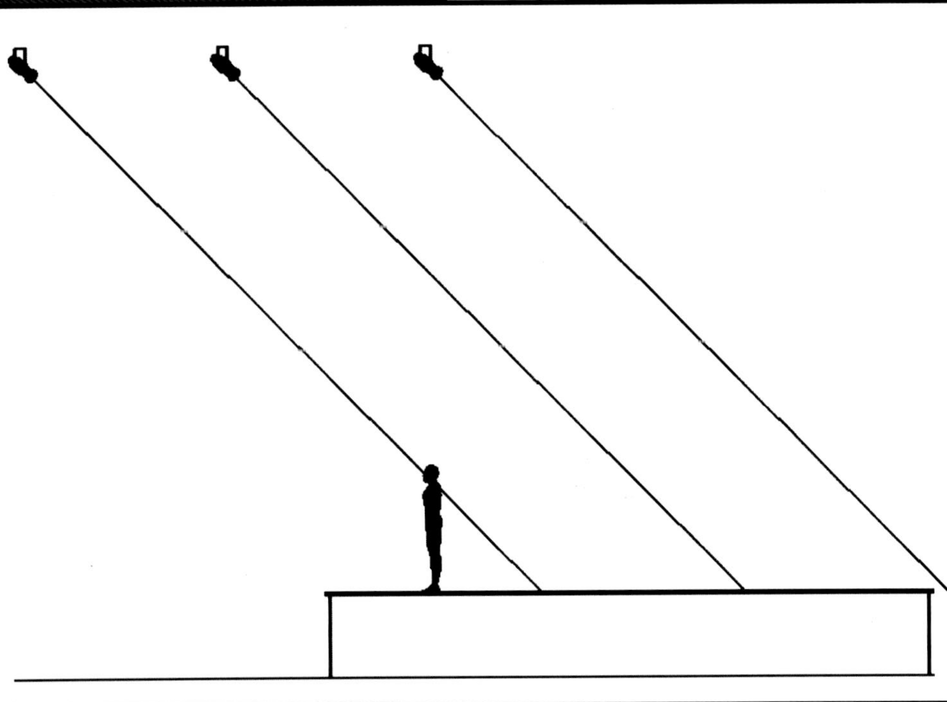

be the key light and the other will be the fill light. Then we will create contrast by toning the key light with a slightly warm color and the fill light with a slightly cool color.

The warm tone in the key lights can be something like as a Roscolux 02, Apollo 7050, Lee 162 or GAM 340 bastard amber gel. The cool tone of the fill light can be something such as a Roscolux 51, Apollo 3200, or GAM 980 surprise pink. The contrast will serve to emphasize the features and expressions of the subject. But if the subject is being captured on video, the contrasting colors may be too strong. Look at the video monitor and change or remove the gels in the fill lights if necessary.

Sometimes it helps to soften the fill light with a light frost filter such as a Rosco 101, Apollo 1050, or GAM 10-50 light frost. Keep in mind that when you add a light frost filter, the intensity drops about 10% to 25% and the field widens. Experience will be the best teacher, and after experimenting a few times you will get a feel for using diffusion and how it affects your results.

For each of the acting areas, the same two-light configuration should be duplicated. We will draw these fixtures in our lighting plot as shown in the illustration. If we're working with a 3D model we need to make sure the height of the instruments is such that the projection angle is no more than 45 degrees from the horizon. When we are finshed we will have a number of fixtures equal to two times the number of acting areas.

RIGGING LOCATION

The final rigging locations of the fixtures might have to be compromised because of the available rigging options. In most cases this is a compromise between the ideal lighting positions and the available rigging positions. Try to locate the rigging under a structural beam so that it can be rigged more easily and it will be structurally sound. In some cases a structural engineer may have to be consulted to insure the safety of the hang.

Remember to take into consideration that the lighting instruments will need to be accessed regularly for focusing and maintenance. Think about how you will reach them if they are located above the pews or high in the ceiling. In some cases a ladder will be sufficient but in others a hydraulic lift might needed to access very high or difficult to reach locations. Adding a catwalk is ideal but it doesn't always fit in the budget.

If the lighting positions need to be adjusted because of the available rigging locations, then a lower horizontal angle rather than a steeper angle will create fewer shadows in the eye sockets and under the nose and jowls (see illustration bottom right). If you have to use a longer throw then you will have to use a lens with a narrower beam angle. The trade-off is that a shallower angle produces more glare in the eyes of the subject and some people with sensitive eyes will object. This is one of the compromises a lighting designer has to make for practical purposes. It would be great if we could locate the key light at eye level, but few people are able to deal with the harsh glare for any length of time.

Regardless of where the rigging ends up, the number of fixtures will be double the number of acting areas. So you can get a rough idea for budgeting of how many key lights and fill lights you need for any platform by dividing the platform into acting areas between eight to ten feet, counting them, and doubling that number. But keep in mind that we haven't discussed backlight, foot lights, color wash, or projections.

BACKLIGHT

Adding one backlight for each acting area fills out our lighting plot and makes it a three-point lighting system. The requirements for backlight are different than those of the key and fill light because the spill is less critical. PAR cans or ERS PAR lights with barn doors work well here. The intensity of the backlight is typically about 50% of the key light, although having the ability to push it higher is useful for certain effects. Backlight serves to highlight the hair and shoulders, giving the subject form and definition. It also helps to separate the subject from the background.

There should be one backlight positioned directly behind and above the subject. Ideally, the backlights should be rigged at a 60 degree angle or higher from the horizon, almost like top light. The steeper the angle, the more the light will creep around in front of the subject and the more highlighting we will see. A high rigging position with a steep angle does two things; it does a better job of defining the shape of the subject and it keeps the light out of the eyes of the front row of the audience. Pay close attention to the cone of the light and how it falls into the front rows. If we are using lighting design software we should be able to place a seated audience member on the front row and look at the beam disbursement to make sure the spill can be controlled effectively. Once we have placed the fixture, turn on the beam and look at a side elevation to see the path of the projection. Make any necessary adjustments by relocating the rigging position of the backlights or by adjusting the focus angle.

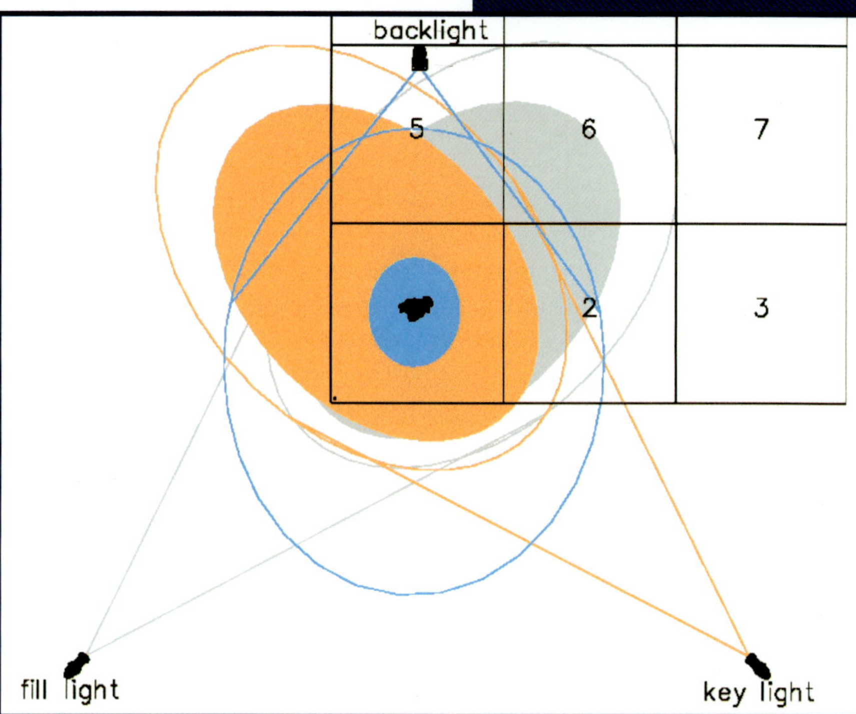

Barn doors can help control the light spill in the audience. Barn doors are an accessory with four large "leafs" that can be adjusted to block and control light spill. They should be adjusted during the focus to prevent the direct projection into the eyes of the audience members.

Add one backlight for each acting area in our plot to make a complete three-

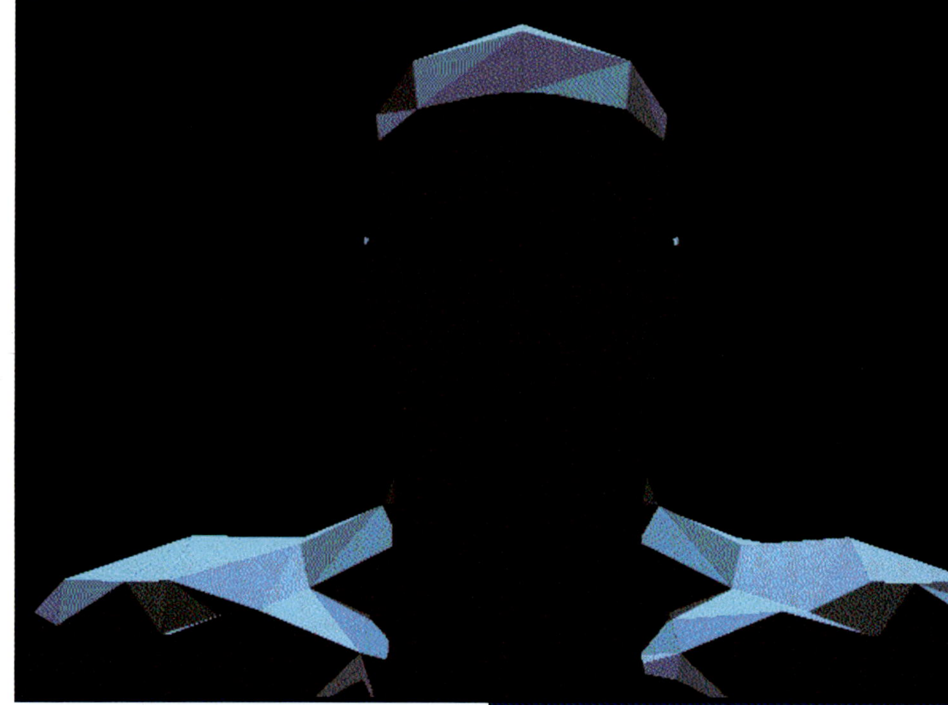

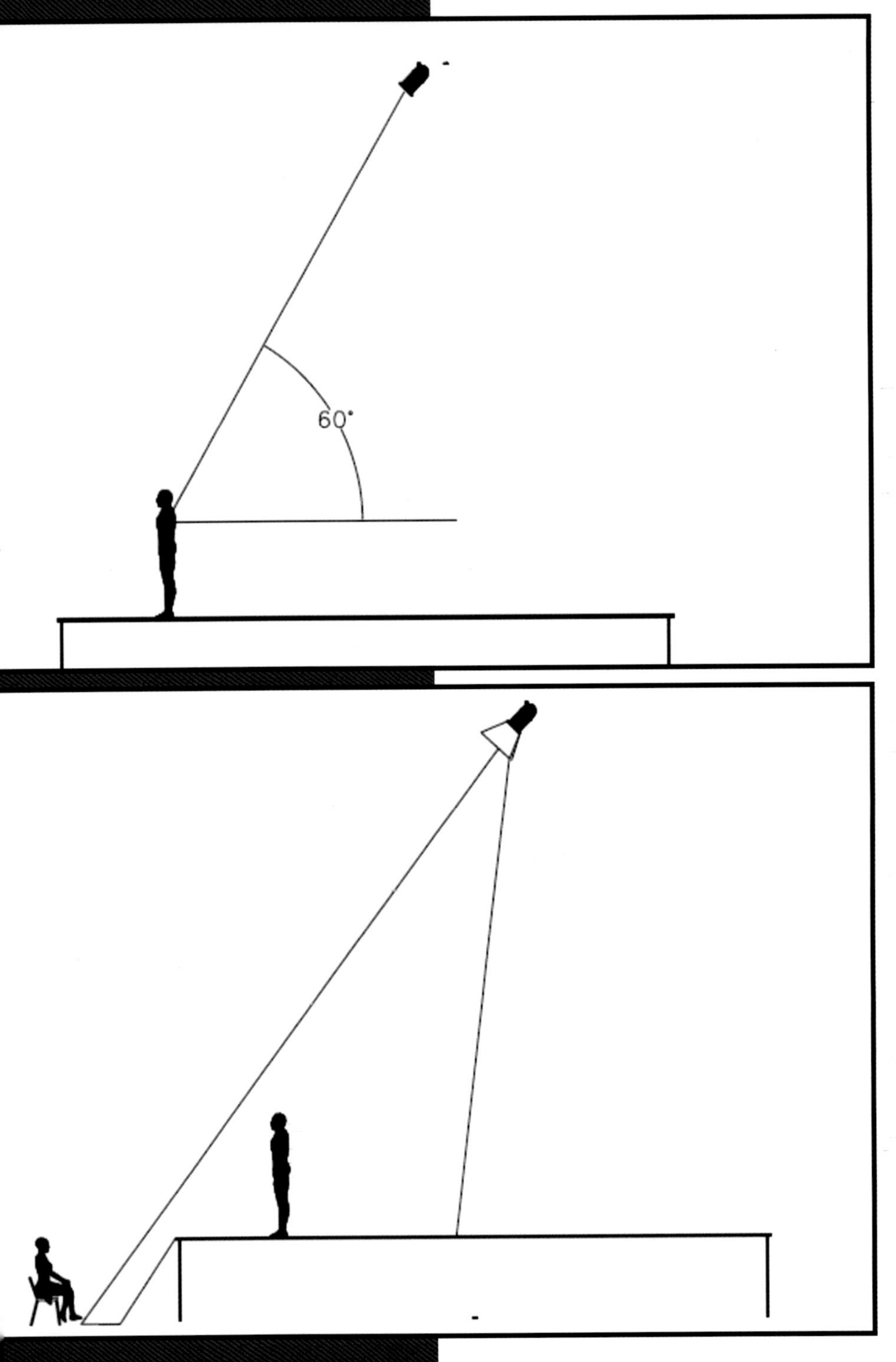

point lighting system. If we can't rig the backlight in the ideal position, cheat the rigging position so that we get a higher rigging angle.

Adding a bluish gel to the backlight helps to better define the separation and make the highlights pop. A Roscolux 60 no color blue or equivalent (Apollo 4750, Lee 202 ½ CTB, etc.) works well for backlight.

Each of these three points of light should be duplicated for every acting area to cover the entire platform. By lighting each acting area individually we have the ability to isolate each area or light the entire platform at once. It also gives us the ability to control where light goes and doesn't go, so we can keep light off of the proscenium, soft goods, set pieces, and any other items that shouldn't have light spill.
The three-point lighting system is not strictly the McCandless method, but it is a variation. But McCandless strived for naturalism, and the three-point lighting

system, in many ways, imitates nature. The key light, like the sun, is direct light, it is strong light, and it is a warm light. The fill light, like reflected sunlight, reflects the cool green shades of the earth. It is less direct and more scattered or diffuse. The backlight, like the sky, projects a bluish tint on the top and back of a subject. Taken together, the three-point lighting system allows us to recreate the naturalism of a bright sunlit day.

The three-point lighting system can be very effective in the right circumstances, but as we will soon see, there are also situations where it is not ideal.

Concepts:

- The McCandless method is an approach to lighting a stage that involves dividing the stage into acting areas, toning the subject with two lights on opposite sides of the subject, both at 45 degree angles from the vertical and 45 degrees above the horizontal, blending the lights from all acting areas, lighting the background and creating special effects.
- The beam angle is the cone produced by a luminaire defined by the angle at which the beam profile drops to 50% of the peak intensity.
- The field angle is the cone produced by a luminaire defined by the angle at which the beam profile drops to 10% of the peak intensity.
- Backlight gives shape, form and definition to the subject and provides separation from the background.
- One backlight should be rigged directly behind each acting area at least 60 degrees above the horizontal.
- Key light can be warmed with a light amber gel like a Roscolux 02, Apollo 7050, or GAM 340 bastard amber.
- Fill light can be cooled and lightly frosted with a Roscolux 51 + Roscolux 101, Apollo 3200 + Apollo 1050, or GAM 980 + GAM 10-50 surprise pink plus light frost.
- Backlight can be tinted with a light blue color such as a Roscolux 60

Words to know:

McCandless method; acting area; photometric data; throw distance; key light; fill light; backlight; frost filter; beam angle; field angle; 3-point lighting; barn doors

Dr. & Mrs. George Bell

Chapter 3

LIGHTING WITH UNIFORMITY

"Light is but the shadow of God."
— Sir Thomas Browne

LIGHTING WITH UNIFORMITY

The first time you ever see your lighting work on a video display, it's an eye-opening experience. That which you thought was so well-lit, evenly illuminated, sufficiently modeled and well defined might turn out to be very different than your eyes lead you to believe.

Video renders light very differently than the human eye because of the differences in the way visual information is sensed, processed, and displayed. It differs vastly from that of the human visual response. Not only do colors appear very differently displayed on a video monitor than they do in real life, but the video camera is also much more sensitive to variations in light levels. The human eye is a truly remarkable instrument that automatically compensates for vast differences in lighting levels. But the video system doesn't have the same ability. Therefore, a video engineer has to monitor the display and adjust the iris of the camera in order to compensate for these variations. But most video engineers would rather not have to rely on constant monitoring and adjustment to produce good work.

One of the biggest challenges facing the lighting designer of a house of worship is creating a video wash with as much uniformity across the entire platform as possible. But it's not as straightforward as it might seem. If we could use a single instrument to illuminate the entire platform then it would be an easy task - just flatten the field and wash the stage with a nicely uniform white light for the video camera.

Unfortunately, it's usually much more complex than that. We typically use multiple light sources in order to control light spill and to isolate certain areas of the platform such as the podium or a soloist in the choir. Even if these weren't issues that we had to deal with, a single source that was powerful enough to illuminate even a medium-sized platform would be very large and unwieldy. For these reasons, we most often choose to use multiple luminaires and blend them as well as we possibly can to create a smooth and uniform video wash.

Most people trained in video production are used to using Fresnels or PAR cans for key light when they want a video wash. But they most often produce video in a studio with a cyc in a very controlled environment. They aren't used to dealing with a live audience, a central subject, a mid-ground,

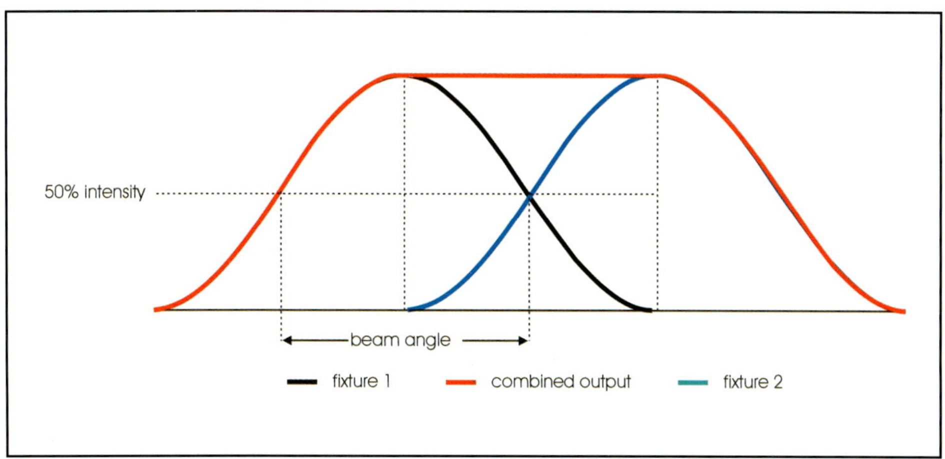

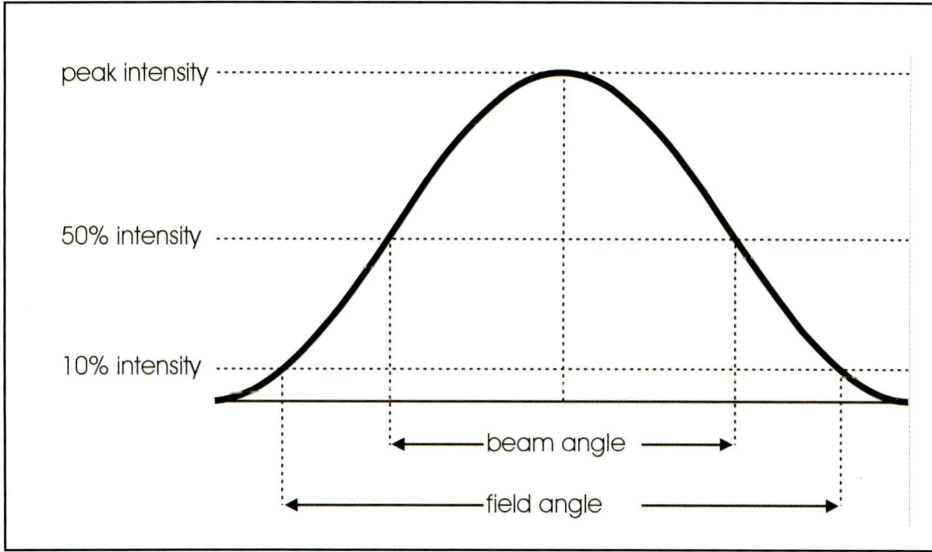

and a choir or other subjects in the background. Many of the lighting techniques used in video production are vastly different than those used in lighting for houses of worship. We use particular instruments for particular reasons and with the right considerations, we can get good results.

BLENDING FIXTURES

Most modern ellipsoidal reflector spotlights (ERS) can be adjusted manually to create a peaked beam or a flat beam. When they are adjusted with a peaked beam, we say that they are optimized for a "cosine distribution" or a "blending distribution." That simply means that the beam profile follows the shape of a cosine. In the ideal profile distribution, the center of the beam peaks at the maximum intensity and it falls off towards the edges as shown in the illustration at the left.

The reason a blending distribution profile is ideal is because when you overlap two fixtures at the 50% drop-off, they produce a uniform field between them. (Red line in illustration above left.)

Notice in the illustration that the two fixtures overlap at point at which the intensity drops to 50% in the beam profile. That is the beam angle (as opposed to the field angle, which is the 10% drop off).

If we then align several fixtures and focus them side-by-side so that they overlap at the beam angle, we can see that the area under the red curve above is perfectly uniform in intensity (excluding the two ends). This illustrates that the beam angle is a useful tool to help calculate the width of a uniform wash when we blend a number of fixtures. We can conclude that, when we blend a number of fixtures, the width of the uniform wash is the diameter of the beam at a given throw distance multiplied by the number of fixtures minus one.

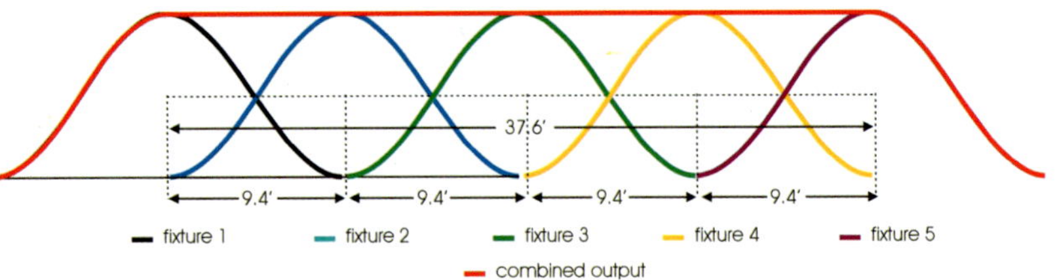

Width of wash = (number of fixtures – 1) x diameter of beam

The graphic above illustrates this formula. There are five fixtures, and the uniform wash is four times the width of the beam of a single instrument. The width of the wash and the diameter of the beam should be in the same units. For example, if we calculate the width of the beam diameter in meters, then the width of the wash will also be in meters. If we use inches instead, then the width will be in inches. This formula provides us with a handy tool to quickly evaluate how many instruments are needed to light a particular area.

PROJECTION AT AN ANGLE

The uniformity created by blending two fixtures with an ideal blending distribution works well when the two fixtures are projected straight onto the subject. But when they are projected at a 45 degree angle, as they are in the McCandless method, then the model breaks down. The 45 degree angle of projection introduces some fall off of the intensity on the far edge of the beam. The fall off follows the inverse square law, which says that the intensity of light falls off exponentially as the throw distance increases linearly.

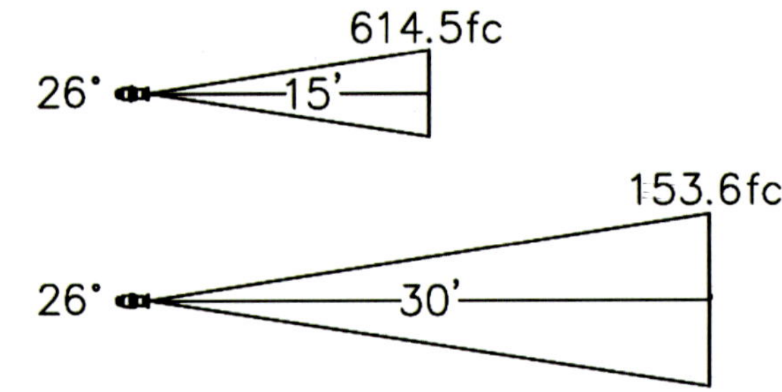

Illuminance = luminous intensity ÷ (throw distance)²

For example, suppose our throw distance is 15 feet and the illuminance is 614.5 footcandles, as shown above. If we double the throw distance to 30 feet, then the illuminance would not drop in half, but it would drop by a factor of four to 153.6 footcandles. So we can see that any change in the throw distance results in an exponential change in the illuminance. When we skew the angle, the throw distance varies from the side to the far side and the illuminance changes across the beam.

The illustration above shows what happens to the illuminance across the front of the subject when we project the light at a 45 degree angle. In this example the throw distance on

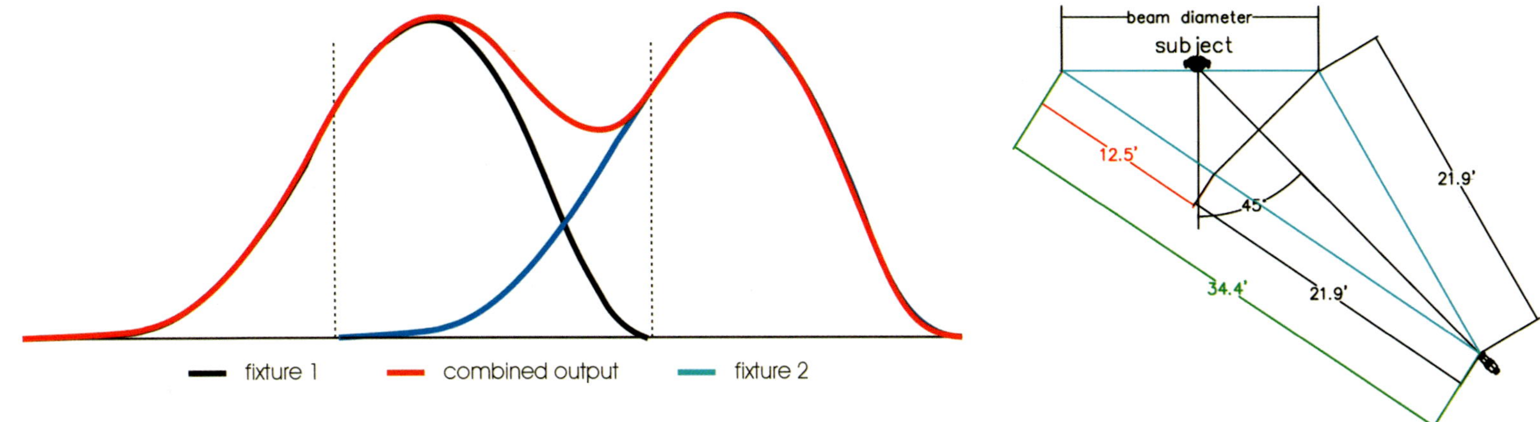

the near side of the beam is 21.9 feet but at the far side of the beam the throw distance is 34.4 feet. That means that the throw distance on the far side of the beam is 12.5 feet longer, or 57% farther, than that of the near side of the beam. In terms of illuminance, we can use the throw distances to calculate the relative difference from the near side to the far side. If we assume the illuminance on the near side is unity (1 unit), then the luminous intensity is 479.6 lumens. The illuminance at the far side of the beam would then be 0.405 footcandles. That's two and a half times less than the near side.

The illustration on the right shows the blending distribution for two fixtures when they are projected at a 45 degree angle. As we can see, the perfect uniformity that we saw in the previous example is lost. Instead, there is a cold spot between fixtures due to the fall-off of the intensity from the near side of the beam to the far. When even more fixtures are blended in this manner, it produces a series of hot spots and cold spots instead of the uniform video wash we saw in the previous example.

LIGHTING FOR VIDEO

To avoid this problem we need to reassess how we set up our key light or video wash and how we design our lighting system. Instead of using a key light and a fill light at 45 degree angles to the subject, we can move the key light so that it projects directly on the subject and relocate the fill light. The logical place to move the fill light is on either side of the subject. This is not the classic McCandless three-point lighting system but a variation of it.

For applications without video, the non-uniformity of the wash created by blending a row of fixtures projected at a 45 degree angle is not critical. It is usually acceptable because the human eye is forgiving and it doesn't see the hot and cold spots as well as a camera does. But in the event that video is involved, this set up can pose problems. For that reason, the 4-point lighting system, where the key light is focused straight on to the subject and two fill lights are located on either side of the subject might a better solution for creating a video wash. We will discuss more about the four-point lighting system and how to design a complete lighting plot with it in the next chapter.

Concepts:

- A cosine or blending distribution is a beam profile with the shape of a cosine curve. An ideal blending distribution provides perfect uniformity when blended two or more luminaires are blended.
- When you blend a number of fixtures with a cosine distribution, the total width of the resulting wash is equal to the number of fixtures minus one, times the diameter of the beam at the given throw distance.
- The inverse square law says that the intensity of light falls off exponentially as the throw distance increases linearly.
- Blending fixtures with a cosine distribution projected at an angle does not produce a uniform wash.

Formulas:

Width of wash (feet) = [number of fixtures -1] x diameter of beam (feet)

Illuminance (footcandles) = luminous intensity (candelas) ÷ [throw distance (feet)]^2

Words to know:

Cosine distribution; blending distribution; inverse square law.

Chapter 4

THE FOUR-POINT LIGHTING SYSTEM

"I want to know God's thoughts,
the rest are details."
—Albert Einstein

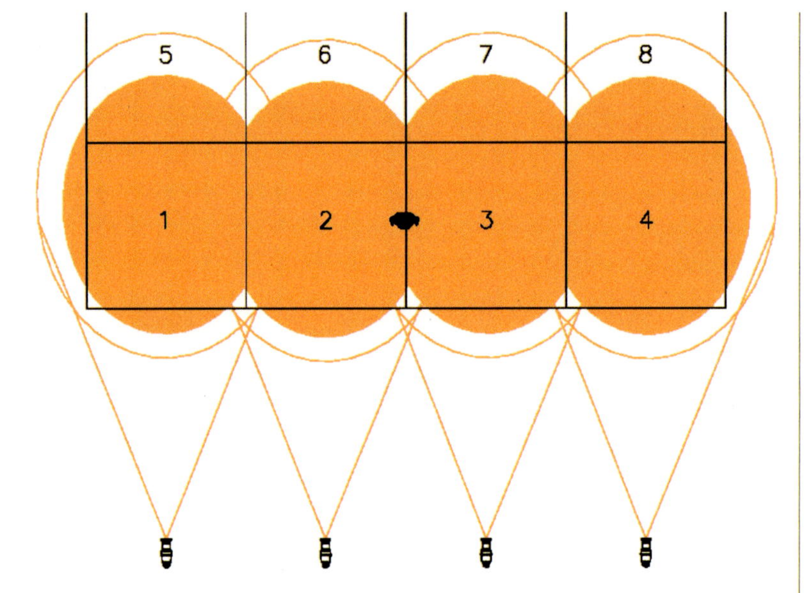

THE FOUR-POINT LIGHTING SYSTEM

If we start with the premise that we can achieve a uniform wash across the front of the platform by blending fixtures with an ideal distribution projected straight onto the stage, then we can adapt the McCandless method to suit a more video-friendly lighting system. Instead of projecting from a 45 degree angle, we simply move all of the key lights so that they are projecting directly onto the platform as shown at the right.

Then we can add the fill light by placing one fixture on either side of each acting area at a 90 degree angle to the key lights. We finish the plot by adding one backlight for each acting area.

The key lights, fill lights, and backlights can be gelled with the same warm, cool, and high color temperature gels we used in the three-point lighting system. We can use the same lighting angles as before; 45 degrees above the horizon.

Note that in a 4-point lighting system, the subject is lit from the front, which tends to produce a flat look. Lighting a subject from an angle brings out the characteristic features of the subject. However, where video is involved, the cameras are typically off-center if there are two stationary cameras. If there are three cameras, then two of the three will be off-center. The result is that most of the cameras see the subject from an angle, so they get the benefit of a uniform front wash as well as the benefit of the modeling of the subject.

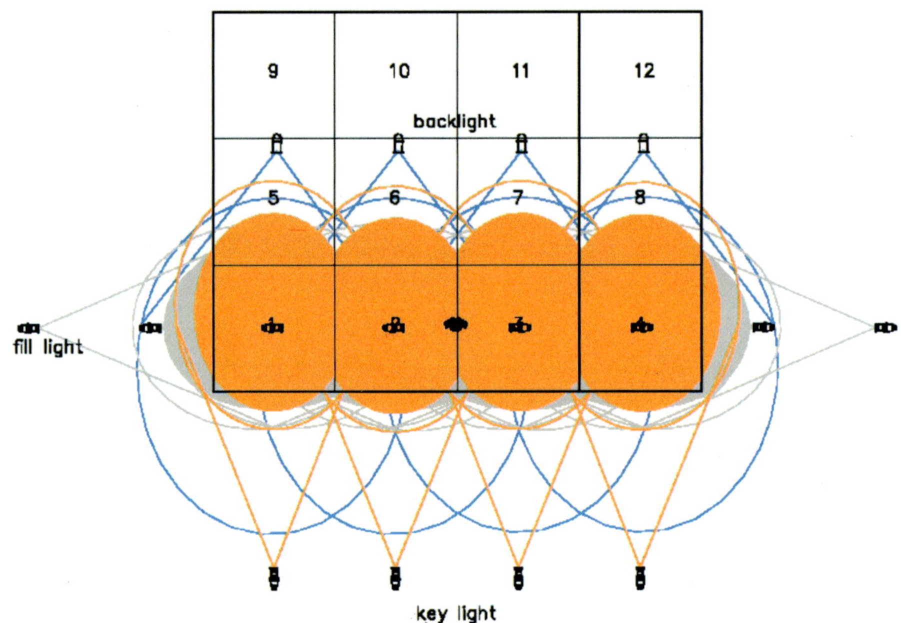

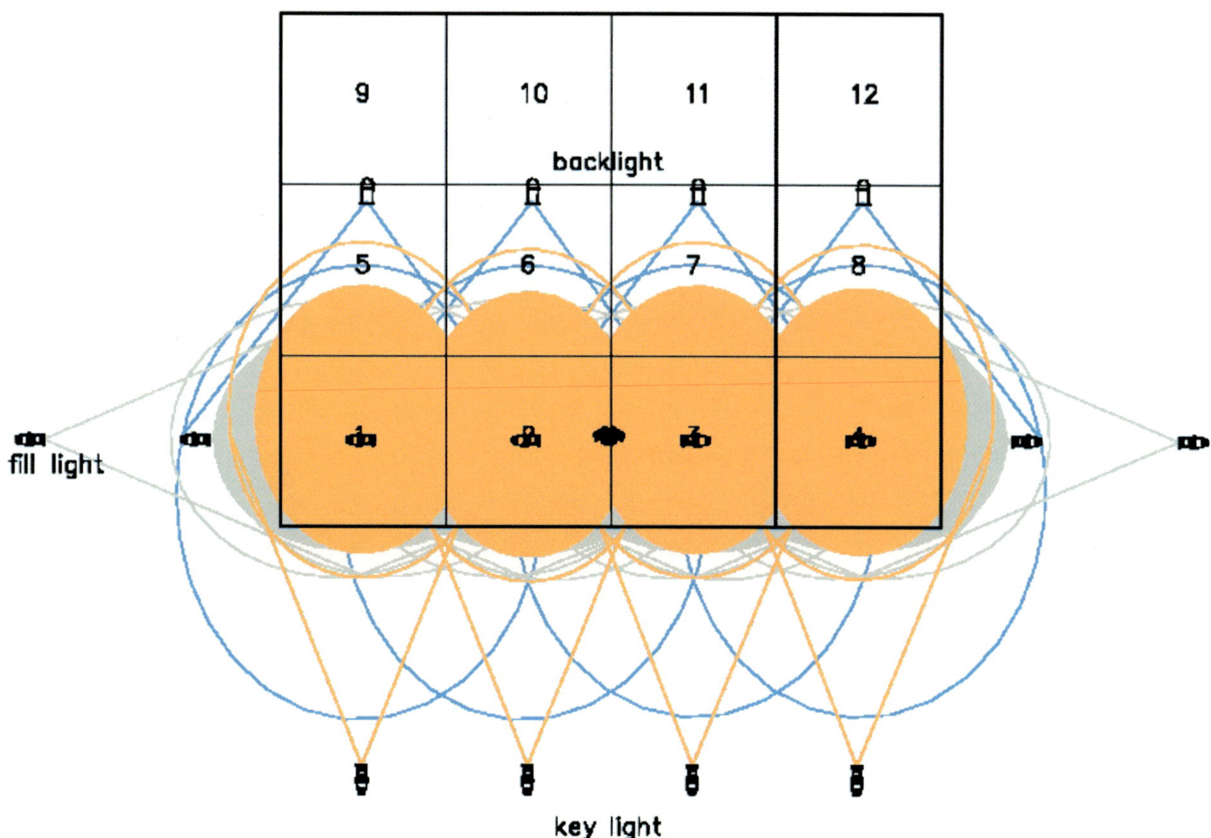

Four points of light or more is sometimes referred to as "jewel lighting" because it makes the subject sparkle like a jewel. In many cases a six- or eight-point lighting system is used in a jewel lighting system.

In the next few chapters we'll talk about how to fully implement a 4-point lighting system. We'll talk about choosing the appropriate luminaires for the project and their exact placement to fit the space.

Concepts:

- A 4-point lighting system (sometimes referred to as jewel lighting) provides more uniformity for video than a 3-point lighting system. It has a front key light, two side fill lights and one backlight.

Words to know:

4-point lighting; jewel lighting.

Chapter 5

SELECTING LIGHT SOURCES

"Think of yourself
as an incandescent power,
illuminated and perhaps forever
talked to by God and his messengers."
— Brenda Ueland

SELECTING LIGHT SOURCES

Now that we understand the main elements of a lighting system, we can consider how to select its components. Before we discuss the selection of lighting fixtures for specific applications, let's consider all the lighting tools available to us.

The types of luminaires from which we will choose for key light, fill light, and back light include PAR cans, ellipsoidal reflector spotlights (ERS), and Fresnels. Automated lights are a special case and are typically either spot fixtures, similar to an ERS, or wash fixtures, similar to a Fresnel fixture. Each of these fixtures has advantages and disadvantages. We'll consider each type and discuss their attributes.

PAR CANS

The parabolic aluminized reflector fixture, or PAR can, is available in a variety of sizes including PAR 16, PAR 36, PAR 46, PAR 56, and PAR 64. The number is a measure of the diameter of the fixture in eighths of an inch, so a PAR 64, for example, is eight inches in diameter. The lamps that fit in a PAR can, with the exception of a PAR 16, are sealed beam incandescent lamps, much like a car headlight, with an integral reflector. They are available in a variety of wattages and lumen output, including long-life versions that last about 2000 hours. PAR lenses that fit on the front of PAR cans are available with a variety of field angles including: very narrow spot (VNSP); narrow spot (NSP); medium flood (MFL); and wide flood (WFL). Most PAR 64s can be purchased with a set of interchangeable lenses.

PAR cans are relatively inexpensive and output a relatively large amount of light. Because there are no optics other than a reflector and the output lens, they lose little light to optical components. The down side is that they have poor uniformity and they image the filament enough to produce slight aberrations in the field. They also have no integral means of controlling light spill. Barn doors can be purchased as an accessory for that purpose.

ERS FIXTURES

The ellipsoidal reflector spotlight is sometimes referred to by the generic name "leko." It was derived from the Century Lighting trade name Lekolite, which was named after its inventors, Joseph Levy and Edward Kook. ETC was the first to introduce an ERS with a compact filament lamp source, which is very efficient compared to the original Lekolite. A 575-watt Source Four ERS produces about the same amount of light as a 1000-watt Lekolite. That not only saves energy, it also produces less heat that needs to be removed by the HVAC (heating/ventilating/air conditioning) system. Other theatrical stage lighting manufacturers have followed suit with their own version of an ERS with a compact filament lamp source including Altman Shakespeare, Colortran Leo, Strand SL Coolbeam, Selecon Pacific, and others.

ERS fixtures in North America are typically used with interchangeable fixed angle lenses as opposed to zoom lenses, which are more common in Europe. They can be used for short throw applications with a wide lens or long throw applications with a narrow lens. The lamps are typically 575-watt or 750-watt compact arc quartz halogen lamps but ERS fixtures are also available with a discharge lamp. In the rear of the fixture is a manually adjustable setting to center the lamp and create a peaked beam or a more uniform flat beam. They also have built-in framing shutters which allow you to control light spill and frame objects and set pieces. On the negative side, ERS fixtures are higher in cost than a PAR can or a Fresnel fixture.

FRESNEL FIXTURES

A Fresnel fixture has a lens, called a Fresnel lens, with a series of stepped, concentric rings that produces a soft, unfocused light. The fixtures range in size from three inches to 24 inches with lamps that range from 150 watts to several thousand watts.

Fresnel fixtures are ideal for providing very soft, unfocused light, and they are relatively inexpensive. They are commonly used in television and film production. But they are extremely inefficient and it can be challenging to use them with anything but a relatively short throw. They are often used with barn doors to control light spill but they are not recommended for throw distances of more than 20 or 30 feet except under very controlled circumstances. They are also such large fixtures that they can easily block the line of sight of the audience and therefore they are not often used for key light except in a studio with no live audience or where the audience is secondary to the cameras.

AUTOMATED LIGHTS

Because of their flexibility, automated lights with remote control of pan, tilt, and other parameters, can fit a variety of applications. They are available with a hard edge beam or a soft edge beam, and sometimes they can provide both. They are typically very efficient because most of them use discharge lamp sources. Some have remote shutters to control light spill. Other features, such as a remote zoom, color changers, and pattern projection make them ideal for most lighting situations. Their main drawback is the price tag, and one automated light fixture can easily cost four to twenty times more than an ERS. But given the right circumstances, a fully automated lighting system can be very effective and efficient. For example, in a situation where the electrical system is at maximum load, it would take several thousand dollars to upgrade it. But it might cost the same amount of money to design a fully automated lighting rig and the efficiency of the system would pay itself back over time. More often, automated lighting is used as a supplement to conventional lighting in order to provide color, projection, and special effects.

KEY LIGHT SELECTION

In order to select a luminaire that will fulfill our requirements for the task at hand, we should first consider how it will be used. High on the list of desired characteristics for key lighting are the following:

- **Meets the illuminance requirements** – We set the minimum acceptable illuminance requirements in the initial phase of our design and now we need to make sure we can meet it by selecting an instrument with enough intensity to produce the desired illuminance at the throw distance we need.
- **Variable lens options to size the beam according to requirements** – The key light should offer a variety of lens options so that we can choose the correct beam angle to cover the acting areas sufficiently.
- **Beam control (shutters and/or barn doors)** – We need to be able to keep light off of the proscenium, certain set pieces, the face of the platform and any other areas that will distract the attention of the audience or skew the perspective of the cameras.
- **Ideal distribution beam profile** – We need to be able to blend the lights to produce a uniform front wash.
- **Good color rendering** – We should be able to produce good skin tones without having to worry about the green-magenta balance.
- **High efficiency** – We want to conserve energy whenever possible, not only for the environment but also to keep down the cost of power distribution (feeder cable, distribution panels, branch circuits, etc.), air conditioning, and labor.
- **Long lamp life** – Most churches don't have the luxury of a catwalk and a full-time staff to continually maintain luminaires.

Notice that a long lamp life is among the list of priorities. Although it is listed last, it is really a very important consideration

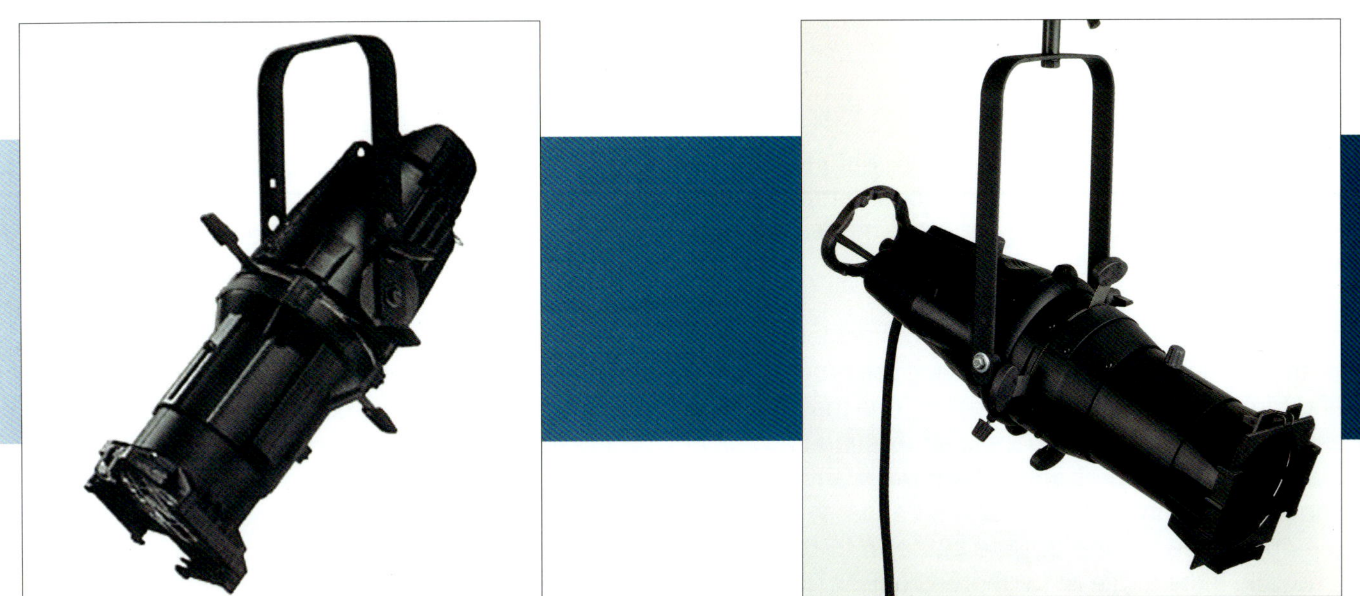

in houses of worship. Given the situation in most churches where the staff is made up of volunteers, it is challenging to keep up with lamp maintenance. Even if there is a catwalk to more easily access fixtures, there are typically enough fixtures in a medium to large lighting system that it can be very time consuming to maintain them all. It is best to specify and use long life lamps, and they are available for almost every type of fixture.

The type of fixture that might best fit our desired characteristics is an ellipsoidal reflector spotlight (ERS). They are designed to provide the illuminance levels we need at the throw distances we will use; they come with interchangeable lenses to size the beam according to requirements; they have shutters to control the beam; most of them have a manually adjustable beam distribution; they use incandescent lamps with high color rendering; and they are among the most efficient (incandescent) luminaires available. There are several ERS fixtures available from various manufacturers that fit our requirements. Those with a dichroic glass reflector are more efficient than those with an aluminum reflector, but they usually come with a price premium.

As previously mentioned, the down side of ERS fixtures is that they are relatively expensive compared to a simple PAR can. On the other hand, they are relatively inexpensive compared to automated lighting. Some people like to use PAR cans for key light because they produce a lot of light (at the expense of your electricity bill and HVAC) and they are relatively easy to blend because they have a soft edge. But the tradeoff is that they need barn doors to control light spill and keep it off of video screens, set pieces, etc., they have no profile distribution control, and they image the filament, which produces aberrations and non-uniformity that can look bad on camera.

CALCULATING THE THROW DISTANCE

Once we have selected the type of fixture we want to use, we need to evaluate its photometric performance to make sure it meets the target illuminance at our required throw distance. But first we have to find that distance.

Keep in mind that we'll be looking for a convenient rigging location for the lighting, one that will provide the correct throw distance and trim (height of the fixtures), and one that will allow easy access for maintenance. If there is an existing catwalk in the sanctuary then that's probably where we want to locate the front lighting. We only need to make sure that we have no more than a 45 degree angle from the platform to the rigging rail in the catwalk. If the angle is 45 degrees or less, then that's where we want to locate the front lighting. All we need to do in that case is to size the lenses accordingly.

But suppose we're working with new construction and it's up to us to decide where to locate the front lighting. In that case we have the opportunity to choose the ideal position and specify the ideal rigging. A little calculation will reveal the ideal position, and the ideal rigging is typically a 1-1/2" schedule 40 black iron pipe rigged below an electrical raceway[1]. That allows us to rig each light on the pipe and plug it into an outlet directly above it, provided the electrical plans with the correct locations have been given to the electricians who install the raceway and pull the wiring. Schedule 40 iron pipe is relatively inexpensive, readily available in most locations, and it's strong enough to support most lighting equipment. The raceway can be supplied by an electrical supply house, a theatrical rigging supplier, or by the electrical contractor.

If the ceiling is open with exposed steel joists and trusses, then we might want to have the raceway and iron pipe rigged directly to the bottom of a joist. We should allow about three and a half feet for the raceway, pipe, and fixture clamp and if we subtract that from the distance from the floor to the bottom of the steel joists (assuming the house is not raked), that will be the trim height of the fixtures.

Now we need to figure out exactly which of the many joists to use. Working backwards from the subject to the rigging location, we will look for the best location. We want the lights to target the chest area and cover the subject from head to toe, so we need to keep in mind that the target is the height of the platform plus the height of the middle of the subject. If the platform is three feet high, we will focus the key light in the center of the acting area and about 7' 6" above the floor (4' 6" above the platform plus the height of the platform).

We now know the elevation (vertical distance from the target to the fixture) is from the subject to the bottom of the red iron joists, minus three and a half feet for the rigging. For example, if it's 26' from the floor to the bottom of the joists, then the fixtures will trim at 22' 6" and the elevation will be 7' 6" less than that, or 15'. And we know we want the projection angle from the horizontal to be 45 degrees. By using the Pythagorean Theorem from trigonometry, we can calculate the throw distance.

---

2 A raceway is a long metal, rectangular enclosure for electrical wire used for electrical power distribution.

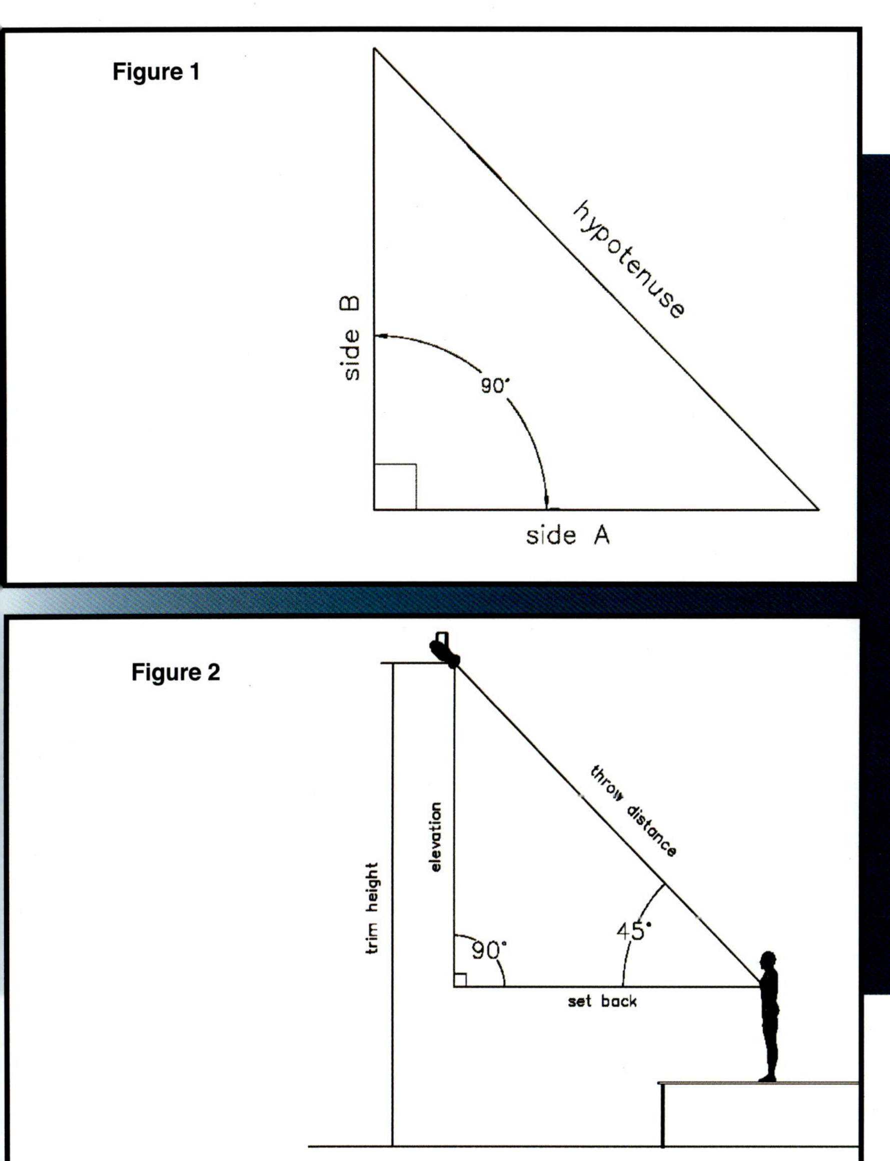

Figure 2 - The throw distance is the hypotenuse, side A is the setback and side B is the elevation.

The Pythagorean Theorem says that the square of the hypotenuse (the side opposite of the right angle) of a right triangle (a triangle with one right angle, or one 90 degree angle) is the sum of the squares of the other two sides.

Figure 1 - Pythagorean Theorem - Hypotenuse^2 = side A^2 + side B^2

For our purposes, the hypotenuse is the throw distance, side A of the right triangle is the setback distance from the subject and side B is the elevation (trim height minus the platform height and the height to the middle of the subject). So our equation becomes:

Hypontenuse^2 = A^2 + B^2
Throw distance^2 = setback^2 + elevation^2

In a 45 degree right triangle the two sides are equal in length. So the setback distance should be equal to the elevation in our set up. We know that our trim height is limited by the ceiling height and we're guessing that we can trim at no higher than 22.5 feet. If we subtract the height of the platform (3') and the height from the platform to the center of the subject (4' 6"), then that gives us an elevation of 15 feet.

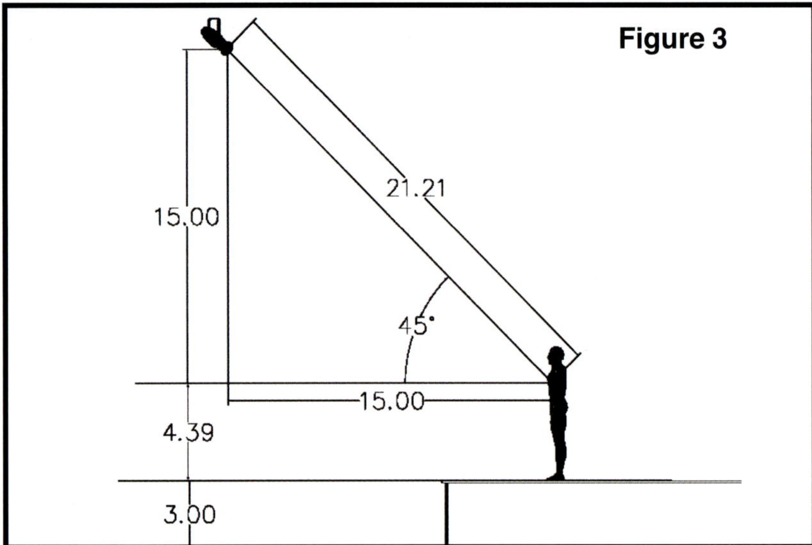

Figure 3 - With a 25' ceiling, the front light might trim at about 22.5',meaning the throw will be less than 20 feet with a three-foot stage.

Now we can plug in some numbers:

$$(\text{Throw distance})^2 = (\text{setback})^2 + (\text{elevation})^2$$

$$\text{Throw distance} = \text{square root } [(\text{setback})^2 + (\text{elevation})^2]$$

$$\text{Throw distance} = \text{square root } [(15)^2 + (15)^2]$$

$$\text{Throw distance} = \text{square root } [2 \times (15)^2]$$

$$\text{Throw distance} = \text{square root } [450]$$

$$\text{Throw distance} = 21.21 \text{ feet}$$

CALCULATING THE ILLUMINANCE

Now that we know our throw distance, we have to find a lens that sufficiently covers the acting area and provides enough illuminance to meet our requirements. Most fixtures have some means of varying the beam and/or field angle. Sometimes the lens is replaceable and sometimes it is an adjustable zoom lens. Either way, we will be looking for a lens or zoom setting that is wide enough to cover the acting area but not so wide that it spills onto the entire platform and everything around it.

Note that we can easily figure the setback distance by subtracting the height of the target off the floor from the trim height. With that bit of information, you should be able to walk into any room, measure the ceiling height, and calculate roughly where the front of house truss should be rigged.

From our example above, we're looking for a lens that provides a 10'-wide beam at about a 21' throw. With a little experience, we will be familiar with which lens sizes are available for the type of fixture we want to use and we will be able to make an educated guess as a starting point for the lens size that will best fit our needs. In this case, we'll start by looking at a 36 degree lens. Why a 36 degree lens? Because 21' is a relatively short throw distance and we happen to know that 36 degrees is a standard lens size for a very common ERS fixture – the ETC Source Four. If we want to use another brand, like an Altman Shakespeare, we would start with a 40 degree lens.

The photometric data for a Source Four 36° can be found on the manufacturer's web site (www.etcconnect.com). It tells us that the candlepower, or luminous intensity, is 82,000 candelas with a 750-watt HPL lamp. But average rated life for that lamp is only 300 hours, which is on the lower end of the scale. If the lights are on an average of 25 hours per week, then they would last an average of 12 weeks, which is far too often to be changing lamps. We would prefer a lamp with a much longer lamp life, so we might choose the HPL 575/115X, which has an average rated life of 2,000 hours.

That's not to say that it's a true average. Lamp manufacturers have their own method of rating lamp life "averages." They set up a sample of lamps, typically about 100 of them, and the run them until 50% of them have failed and they record the time it took to reach that condition. That's what they use as the average lamp life.

As with most things in life, there is a tradeoff that comes with choosing a lamp with longer life. Longer life lamps also come with a lower luminous intensity, so we have to account for that in our illuminance calculations. If we look at the photometric data for the HPL 575/115X lamp, it gives us a multiplying factor (MF) of 0.66. That means that the luminous intensity figure given has to be de-rated by a factor of 0.66, so the luminous intensity for that lamp is actually 54,120 candelas.

Luminous intensity is a measure of how strong a light is in a certain direction. It's related to the illuminance, but it's not the metric we're looking for. We need to calculate the illuminance, which is a measure of how much light is falling on a certain area at a given throw distance, by using the inverse square law.

Illuminance (footcandles) = luminous intensity (candelas) ÷ [throw distance (feet)]^2
Illuminance = 54,120 ÷ (21.21)^2
Illuminance = 120.3 footcandles

The calculation is based on ideal conditions with a new lamp at rated voltage. In practice, lamps lose light output as they age. The quartz envelope of the lamp gradually loses its crystalline structure through repeated heating and cooling cycles and becomes opaque. This is known as devitrification. There is also a voltage drop in the circuit feeding the lamp, although the rated voltage of 115V accounts for that. But the longer the circuit, the greater the voltage drop. And if the voltage at the lamp is less than the rated voltage, the light output drops exponentially.

Therefore, it is a good idea to take this into account and de-rate our illuminance calculation by 10% or 20%. Still, that gives us between 96 and 108 footcandles, so we have to decide if that's sufficient for our purposes. If not, then we have several options: we can change to a more narrow lens and add more acting areas to compensate; we can switch to the shorter life 575-watt lamp with more luminous flux; we can switch to a more powerful 750-watt lamp (although these are not available in a longer life version); or we can double up on fixtures and use two key lights for each acting area. The last option, albeit more expensive, is a good fail-safe measure. It provides redundancy so that in the event that one lamp fails during a service then you still have some light on the subject. If we decide that we can live with 96 footcandles after de-rating the illuminance calculation, then we will accept the 36 degree lens and move on.

In some cases the photometric data is provided in the form of a chart instead of the total luminous flux. These charts typically show the illuminance and beam width or field width at periodic throw distances, e.g., 10 feet, 20 feet, 30 feet, etc. If it shows the exact throw distance we happen to be looking for then it's easy to evaluate our luminaire and lens choice. If not, then we can either extrapolate, or we can work backwards from one of the data points to calculate the total luminous flux and then work forwards to calculate the illuminance.

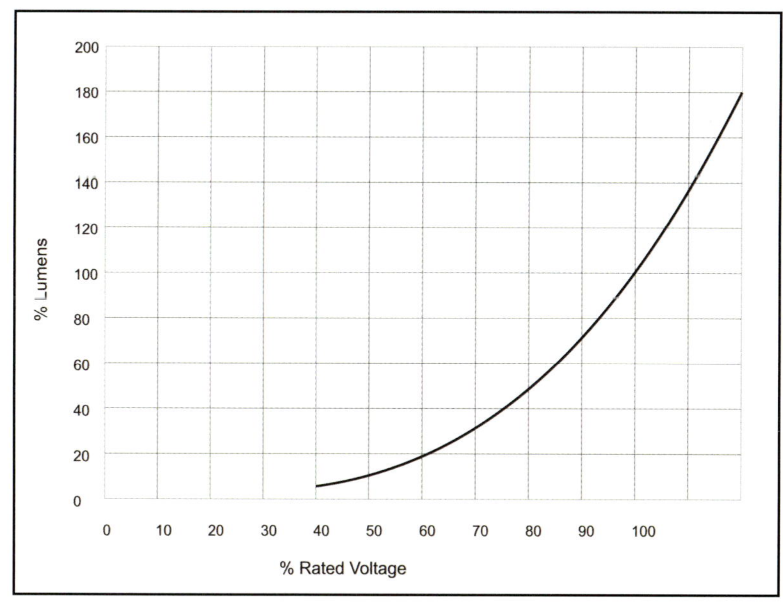

Fig. voltage versus lumens

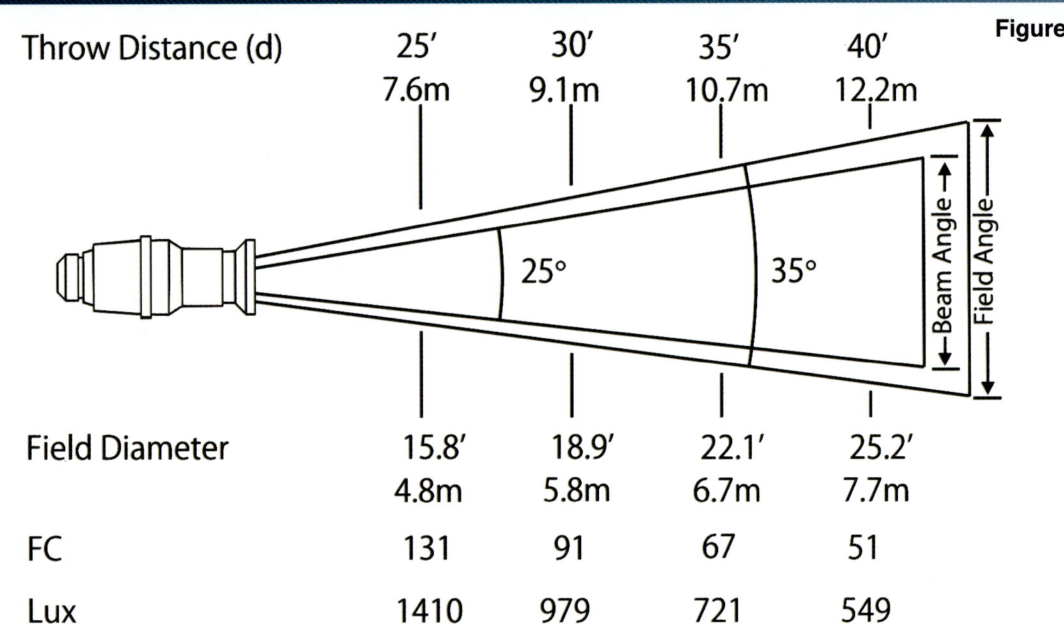

Figure 4 - Photometric chart showing field diameter and illuminance at periodic throw distances. You can use the inverse square law to convert the given data to any throw distance.

Suppose, for example, a photometric chart indicates that the illuminance is 131 footcandles and the field width is 15.8' with a throw of 25'. But we want to know the illuminance and field width with a throw distance of 21.21'.

By using the inverse square law, we can figure out the total luminous flux:

Illuminance (footcandles) = luminous intensity (candelas) ÷ [throw distance (feet)]^2
Luminous intensity = illuminance × (throw distance)^2
Luminous intensity = 131 × (25)^2 = 81,875 candelas

If we looked at the photometric data on the manufacturer's web site, we may have noticed that we could have taken a short cut. We could have, for example, used the multiplier .45, taken straight from the photometric data, to calculate the beam diameter at any distance [2 x Tan(12.5°) = .45].

By the same token, if we are using a CAD design software tool like WYSIWYG, LD Assistant or VectorWorks, then the software will do some of the calculations for us. But regardless of the tools you have at your disposal, we should know how to derive the calculations. Once we understand the relationship between the lighting metrics, we can develop an intuitive feel for the numbers and our design will go much faster and turn out much better.

How ever we arrive at the answer, once we know the luminous intensity, then we can figure out the illuminance at the throw distance in which we're interested.

Illuminance (footcandles) = luminous intensity (candelas) ÷ [throw distance (feet)]^2

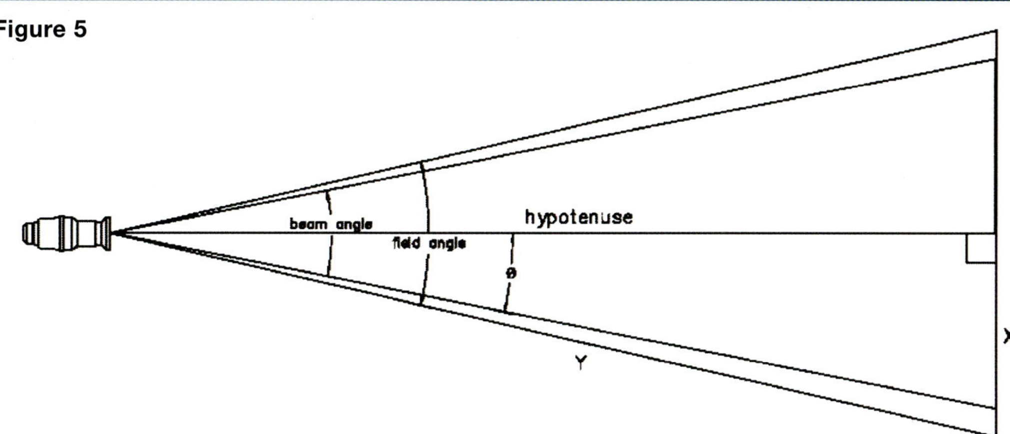

Figure 5 - By drawing a line down the center of the beam we can create two right triangles in order to find the field diameter at a given throw distance.

Illuminance = 81,875 ÷ (21.21)²
Illuminance = 182 footcandles

"Again, if we choose to use a long life lamp, then we need to de-rate this figure using the multiplying factor. Therefore, we would end up with about 120 footcandles before accounting for lumen decreciation."

CALCULATING THE BEAM WIDTH

Next we need to check to make sure the lens we are considering covers the acting area sufficiently. Ideally, we want the beam width to be the same width as the acting area so that when it overlaps with the adjacent beam it will cover the area uniformly. If we can't match it exactly then it's better to make it slightly wider than to make it slightly narrower because that will provide better uniformity across the platform.

We can use a simple trigonometric formula to calculate the beam diameter since we know the throw distance and the beam angle of the fixture we selected. The formula we'll use is one for tangents. The tangent of an angle is equal to the side opposite the angle divided by the adjacent side of the triangle.

Tangent Ø = opposite side ÷ adjacent side

Notice that the formula only works for a right triangle. But the beam angle of a luminaire is not a right triangle. We can, however, turn it into two right triangles by drawing a line down the middle of the beam as shown in the illustration.

Now we have two equal right triangles, each of which is half the beam angle of the lens we are considering. If we now look at the photometric data we can find the beam angle for a Source Four 36° fixture, which is 25 degrees (the field angle is 35 degrees). Using the formula for tangents, we can now plug in the values for the angle and the adjacent side. Notice that the adjacent side is our throw distance. (You'll need a calculator with trigonometric functions to do this calculation.)

Tangent Ø = opposite side ÷ adjacent side
Tan (1/2 beam angle) = X ÷ throw distance
X = Tan (12.5°) × 21.21'
X = 4.7 feet

Note that the value of X is only half the beam diameter, so we need to multiply it by 2 to arrive at the final value.

Beam diameter = 2 × X = 9.4 feet

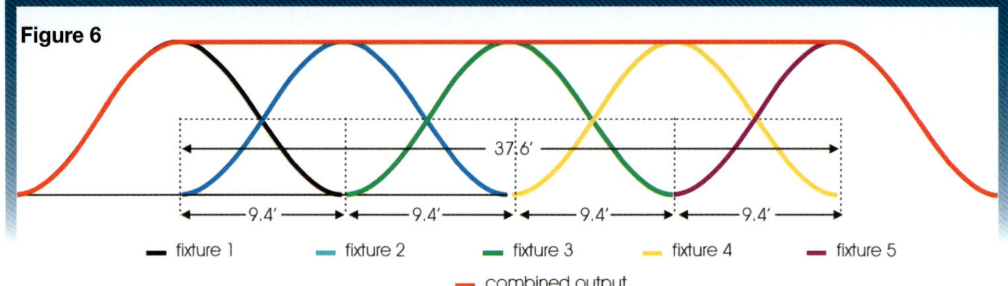

Figure 6 - Five fixtures with an ideal blending distribution and a beam width of 9.4' will cover 37.6' uniformly.

Concepts:

- The Pythagorean Theorem, which defines the relationship between the length of the sides of a right triangle, can be used to find the throw distance if we know the trim height and the height of the platform.
- Given the throw distance and the luminous intensity, we can use the inverse square law to calculate the illuminance.
- When we use the manufacturer's photometric data, we should take into account lumen maintenance due to devitrification and de-rate our calculations.
- The formula for tangents can be used to find the beam diameter at a given throw distance.

Formulas:

Throw distance² = setback² + elevation²

Illuminance (footcandles) = luminous intensity (candelas) ÷ [throw distance (feet)]²

Tangent Ø = opposite side ÷ adjacent side

Words to know:

Ellipsoidal reflector spotlight (ERS); dichroic; trim height; Pythagorean Theorem; hypotenuse; right triangle; setback; elevation; candlepower; luminous intensity; devitrification; de-rate; tangent; raceway.

CALCULATING UNIFORM COVERAGE

In the above example, we can cover 9.4 feet uniformly at about 120 footcandles (with new lamps) for every x number of fixtures minus one. For example, five of these lights at this throw would give us 37.6' of uniform coverage [(5 -1) x 9.4' = 37.6'].

If we have a 40-foot-wide platform, then we would need more than five front lights to cover it completely. Therefore, we have a design decision to make; we can either use six fixtures and shutter cut the spill on either side of the platform, or we can use five fixtures and sacrifice some uniformity at the extreme ends of the platform. In this case, since five fixtures will cover 37.6' uniformly, 1.2' on either end of the platform will have some fall-off. It might be a safe bet that the subject won't spend a lot of time standing in the outer 1.2' of the platform. If so, then the fall-off outside of the peak of the beam, which is 4.7 feet (half of 9.4), will illuminate them. So five Source Four 36° fixtures will probably supply enough illuminance and uniform wash for the job and cover the front light.

Alternatively, we could move the FOH truss back to widen the beam enough to cover the entire platform uniformly. But we have to be mindful of the inverse square law because the intensity will drop off exponentially as we increase the throw distance. To calculate how far we would have to move the truss back to cover 40' of the platform uniformly, we start with the formula for tangents. But this time instead of plugging in the value for half of the beam angle and the throw distance, we need to plug in the value for half of the beam angle and half of the desired beam diameter. That's because we know that to cover a 40' platform we want to use five lights with a 10' beam diameter. We begin as follows:

Tangent Ø = opposite side ÷ adjacent side

Tan (½ beam angle) = (½ beam diameter) ÷ throw distance
Throw distance = (½ beam diameter) ÷ Tan (12.5º)
Throw distance = (5') ÷ .22 = 22.6 feet

Now that we know the throw distance we can use the Pythagorean Theorem to find the setback distance.

(Throw distance)² = (setback)² + (elevation)²
Setback = square root [(throw distance)² – (elevation)²]
Setback = square root [(22.6)² – (15)²]
Setback = square root [283.5]
Setback = 16.8'

So by moving the FOH truss back 1.3' from a 15' setback to a 16.8' setback we can increase the beam width to 10'. Now let's check to see how that affected our illuminance by using the inverse square law.

Illuminance (footcandles) = luminous intensity (candelas) ÷ [throw distance (feet)]²
Illuminance = 54,120 ÷ (22.6)²
Illuminance = 106 footcandles

Comparing it to our previous result of 120.3 footcandles, we can see that we lost 14.3 footcandles, an amount that is almost imperceptible to the human eye. Again, to account for lumen depreciation, we should de-rate the illuminance by about 10% to 20%. We end up with 84.8 to 95.4 footcandles. If we're happy with that figure then we can move on. Otherwise, it's back to the drawing board.

It is important to note that increasing the setback decreases the vertical angle of projection, which changes the look of the lighting. Remember, a lower angle of projection reduces the size of the shadows in the eye sockets and under the nose and jowls.
But it's not a good idea to decrease the setback and move the lights closer to the platform with the same trim height because that would increase the vertical angle of projection to more than 45 degrees. That would create problems with harsh shadows. Also, remember not to decrease the angle too far below 45 degrees because the glare will fatigue the eyes of the subject and it will place shadows on the backdrop.

SUMMARY

To summarize, these are the steps we took to select our front light and locate it in the plot:

1. We estimated the maximum trim height we could achieve given our ceiling height and the overhead for the rigging.
2. We selected a fixture to use as a starting point for our design.
3. We used the Pythagorean Theorem to calculate the throw distance based on the trim height with a 45 degree projection.
4. We looked up the luminous intensity (candelas) in the photometric data on the manufacturer's web site and used the inverse square law to calculate the illuminance at our throw distance.
5. We looked up the beam angle in the photometric data and calculated the beam diameter at our throw distance using the formula for tangents.
6. We evaluated the data to see if it fit our calculation and found that it was close.
7. We adjusted the setback to match the width of the platform and recalculated the illuminance at the new throw distance.

Concepts:

- If we know the beam angle and the beam width at a given throw distance, we can determine how many lights would be needed to uniformly cover the stage with front light.

Words to know:

Shutter cut; front of house (FOH); lumen depreciation; computer-aided design (CAD); WYSIWYG; LD Assistant; VectorWorks.

Figure 7

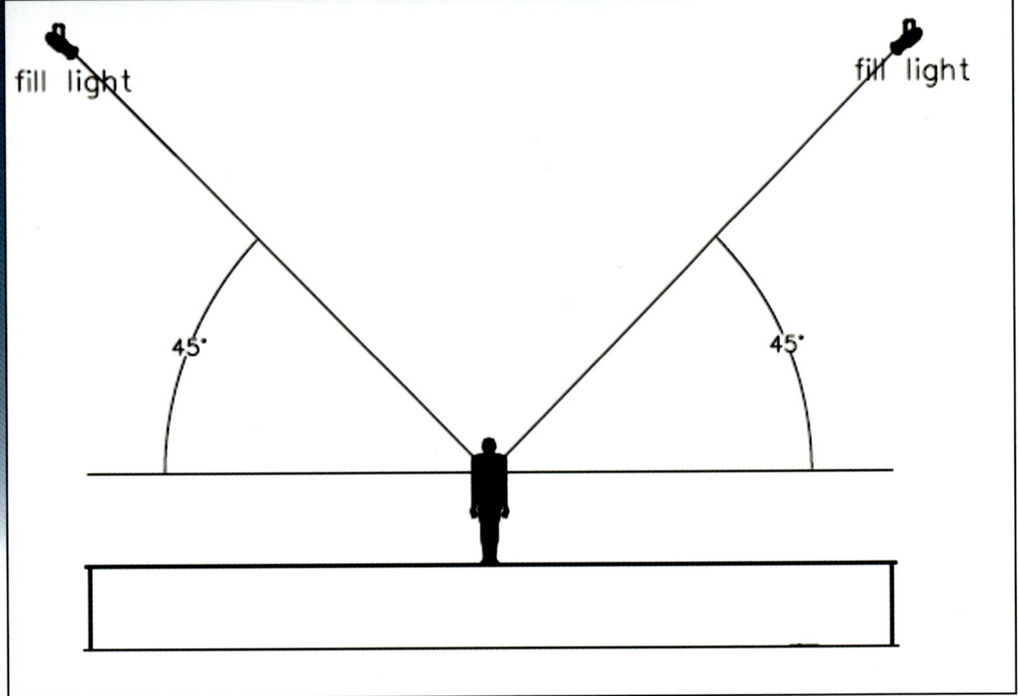

Concepts:

- In a 4-point lighting system, two fill lights should be located on either side of the subject at a 90 degree angle to the front light and 45 degrees above the horizon.
- The backlight should be located directly behind the subject and at least 60 degrees above the horizontal.

Figure 7 - In a 4-point lighting system, the fill light should be located on either side of the subject at a 90 degree angle from the front light and 45 degrees above the horizon.

SELECTING FILL LIGHTS

In a 4-point lighting system, each acting areas should have two fill lights, one on either side of the platform at a 90 degree angle to the key light. Ideally, the fill lights will be located at a 45 degree or lower vertical angle from the horizon.

The fill lights can be the same type of lights that we use for the key light. But the lenses should be sized accordingly, so that the illuminance and beam width fit the throw distance. The purpose of the fill lights is to soften the shadows created by the key lights, and the illuminance can be equal to or slightly less than the key lights. Adding frost filters to the fill lights softens the edge and helps blend them with the key light. Remember that when you use a frost filter it drops the intensity and widens the field angle. How much the intensity drops and the field widens depends on the type of frost filter used.

SELECTING BACKLIGHTS

The uniformity and beam control are not as critical with backlighting, so PAR cans or compact filament PARs (e.g., ETC Source Four PAR) work well for this application. They are relatively inexpensive, readily available, rugged and lightweight. For most any lighting design, whether it's a 3-point or a 4-point lighting system, each key light should have one backlight located directly behind the subject opposite the front light, and they should be rigged at a 60 degree angle, or higher, from the horizon. Remember to use barn doors to prevent light spill onto the first few rows of the audience.

PUTTING IT ALL TOGETHER

In our 4-point lighting plot, as shown below, the fill lights are located in rows parallel to the lip of the platform and centered over the acting areas.

In a television studio or a theatre there might be a pipe grid to accommodate a hang like this, but in a sanctuary we have to be more concerned about lines of sight and aesthetic appearance. Consequently, we often have to compromise our hanging positions to suit the needs of the congregation. We can modify the lighting plot to accommodate a simplified rigging system by consolidating our lighting positions and reduce the number of rows of truss. By moving all of the key lights on the second FOH truss (closer to the platform) to the first FOH truss (farther from the platform) and moving all of the backlights on the upstage truss (the top truss in this plot) to the next closest truss, we can reduce our truss count from six to four, as shown in the figure below.

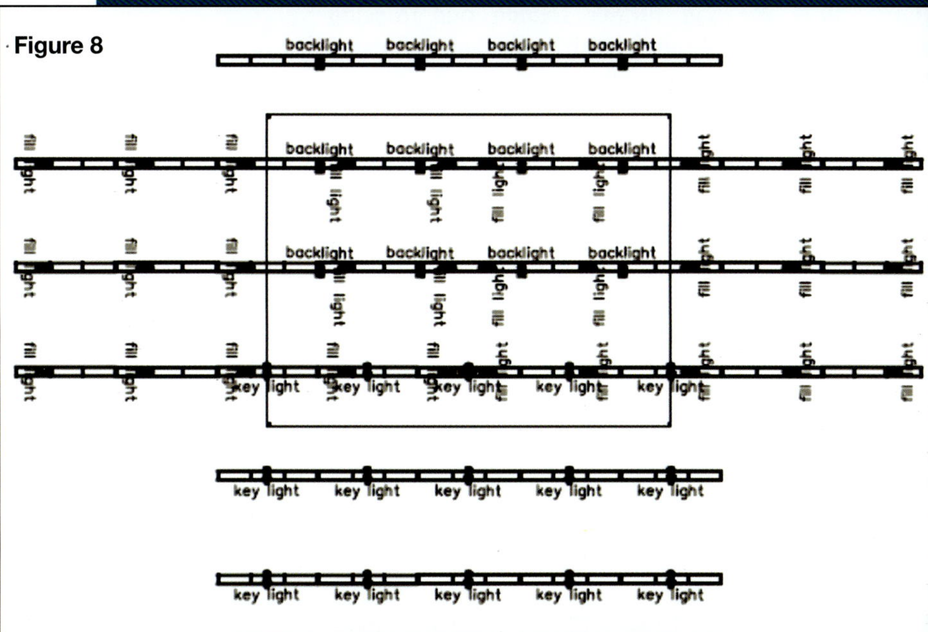

Figure 8 - If we locate our fill lights on either side of the subject at a 90 degree angle to the key light and a 45 degree angle above the horizon, we end up with a row of fill lights parallel to the lip of the platform, one for each row of acting areas.

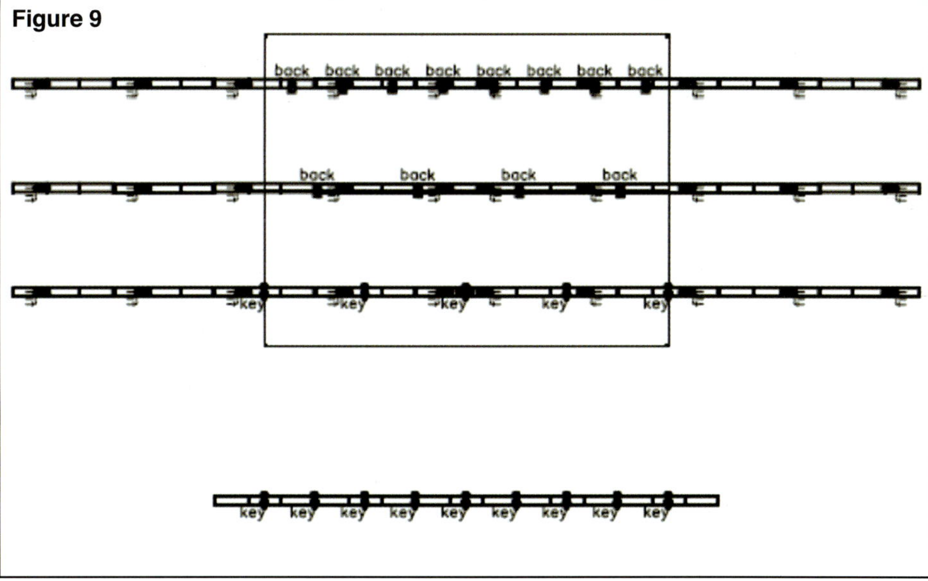

Figure 9 - The 4-point lighting system using six truss positions in the figure above can be consolidated on four spans of truss as shown here.

Figure 10 - We can further reduce our trussing requirements in a 4-point lighting system by using side truss positions stage right and stage left. This is a common lighting plot used in many productions.

We can eliminate more truss by adding side positions stage right and stage left and moving the fill light off the platform. This is a common lighting configuration that you might see in a number of sanctuaries.

In this configuration the fill lights are not at a perfect 90 degree angle, they are throwing a longer distance, and they are at a lower angle than 45 degrees above the horizon. As it turns out, the lower angle doesn't adversely affect the subject because it's side light and not front light. In addition, it helps model the subject better. In many ballet productions, the side light is parallel to the stage because it better accentuates the human form. If the fill lighting positions have to be cheated, cheat them more downstage than upstage. If they are rigged past the 90 degree mark relative to the subject, then they become backlight and not fill light.

Since the throw distance is longer from the side truss positions, the lens sizes should be re-evaluated to determine whether or not they should be changed. Keep in mind that the intensity of the fill light can be less than that of the key light by about 25% to 50%.

Figure 10

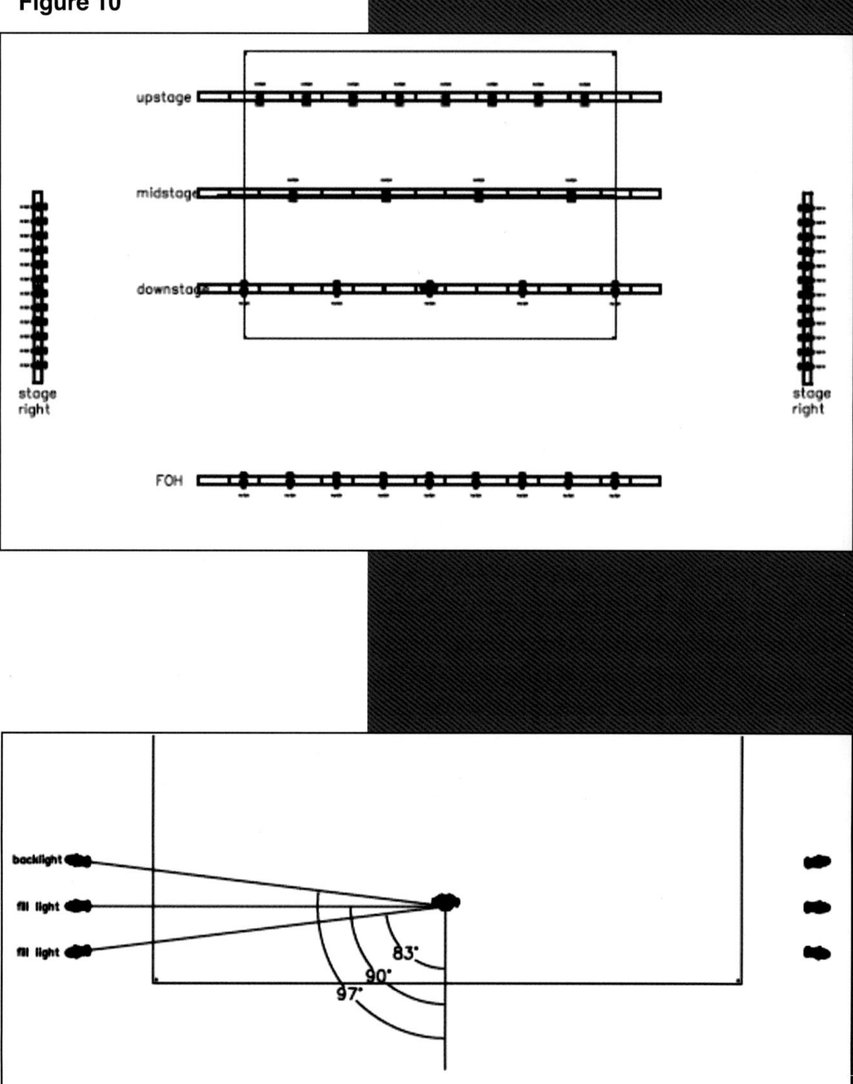

Figure 11

Figure 11 – Repositioning the fill light by moving them downstage is acceptable; moving them upstage makes them more of a backlight.

Figure 12

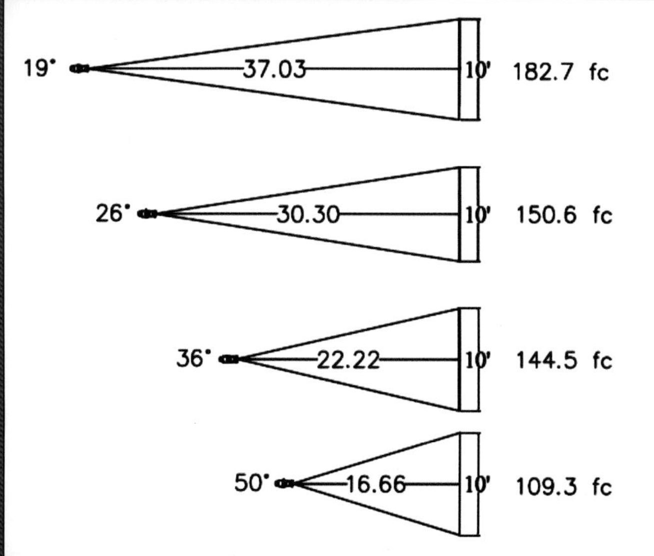

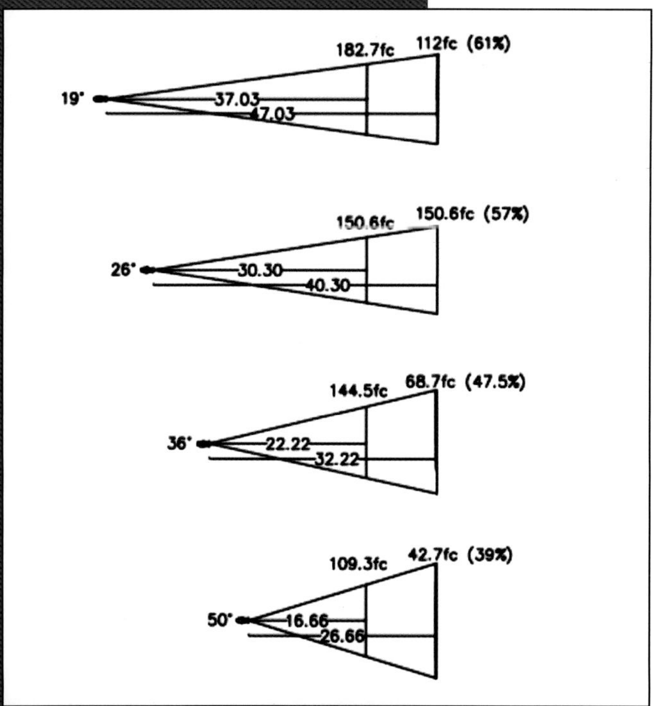

Figure 13

Figure 12 - In theory, the same fixture and lamp with a variety of lenses and throw distances should yield the same illuminance when it is distributed over the same area. But in practice we find that the wider the lens, the less efficient the instrument is.

TWEAKING THE PLOT

When we relocate our lighting positions, we have to take care to resize the lenses to maintain the required beam diameter and illuminance. In theory, resizing the lens to match the original beam size with a different throw distance should yield the same illuminance because of the conservation of energy. The conservation of energy says that energy can neither be created nor destroyed; it can only change forms. In this case, we use the same amount of light, which is a form of energy, and we are using a different lens to project it a longer way. But as long as the beam ends up with the same diameter, then the same amount of light is distributed over the same area.

In practice, however, we find that the inefficiency of the optics comes into play; in general, the wider the beam angle, the less efficient the optics. Consequently, we end up with some variation in the output that is dependent on the lens angle, as illustrated below. Note that each of the fixtures has a different beam angle and a different throw distance, but the beam diameter is the same in each case. In a perfect world we would expect the illuminance to be equal, but the optics are less efficient as the beam angle gets wider.

Figure 13 - The fall off in intensity at a fixed distance behind the subject becomes less pronounced as the throw distance increases.

MAKING ADJUSTMENTS

When we are evaluating how to adjust our light plot, we need to keep these things in mind:

- By increasing the throw distance the beam size will also increase, and when it comes to front lighting, excessive overlapping with the adjacent lights produces a more uniform wash than insufficient overlapping.
- The inverse square law says that as you increase the throw distance, the intensity will fall off exponentially. That helps give us separation between the foreground and the background because the background has less illuminance than the foreground. However, as we increase the throw distance, the difference in intensity between the foreground and the background becomes less pronounced. That's because the ratio of the separation distance to the throw distance is much smaller than when the throw distance is short. So a short throw distance provides more background separation than does a long throw.
- If we can't rig a light in the ideal position and we have a choice between a shorter throw distance and a longer throw distance, then the trade-offs to consider are: glare, harsh shadows, separation of the background, lens efficiency, and overlapping.

CONCLUSION

Understanding the McCandless method of 3-point lighting and how to adapt it for a 4-point lighting system for video is crucial to understanding lighting design. Once we master the fundamentals then we can begin to apply them to real life situations and adapt them to your unique circumstances.

Up until now, we have talked about designing for visibility, modeling, uniformity and to meet the illuminance requirements. These are the broad strokes of lighting design. In subsequent pages in this book we will cover the more esoteric aspects of lighting design. Remember that lighting design is not an exact science and these are principles and guidelines to help us get the most out of a lighting system. It's up to us to study, understand and internalize these principles and use them in creative ways to make them work for our application.

Concepts:

- Sometimes the ideal lighting positions have to be compromised by consolidating truss positions for the sake of line of sights and aesthetics.
- Lighting positions can be moved to accommodate the rigging with little consequence as long as the lens size is reevaluated for coverage and illuminance and close attention is paid to the angles of projection.
- Moving fill light downstage is acceptable; moving fill light upstage and beyond a 90 degree angle from the front light makes it a backlight.
- Energy can neither be created nor destroyed, but it can change forms.
- The wider the beam angle, the less efficient the optics.
- Increasing the throw distance is preferred to decreasing the throw distance as long as the minimum acceptable illuminance is met.
- Excessive beam overlapping is preferred to insufficient overlapping as long as the minimum acceptable illuminance is met.
- A short throw gives better separation between the foreground and the background.

COMPLETING THE LIGHTING PLOT WITH DIFFUSION, COLOR AND AESTHETICS

"It is fully practical to create that which has form in the silence.
The noise art makes is usually heard by
those whose lives listen to God.
It is not advisable to cheat that which has no
other stake than the deeps and brights of all man."
— Kenneth Patchen

Chapter 6

Figure 14 – Production values vary according to the type of service. The carefully crafted look of a traditional service is very different than the look of a contemporary service (inset).

COMPLETING THE LIGHTING PLOT WITH DIFFUSION, COLOR AND AESTHETICS

In the first part of this book, we developed a methodical approach to creating a light plot based on the McCandless lighting method and adapted it to better accommodate video production, thus arriving at the "jewel" lighting method. We talked about which lighting instruments to use and where to use them, how many to use, and how to create a uniform stage wash for audience visibility and for video. Much of what we have already covered involves the more mechanical, formulaic aspects of lighting design – the quantity of light, uniformity and direction of a multi-point lighting system. We began by identifying our design goals and then set about exploring solutions for achieving those goals. We discussed the measurement of light, defined the quantity of light we need, and then set about exploring three-point and four-point lighting design solutions.

In this continuation of the lighting design process, we'll move beyond the issue of mechanics and more into the psychological aspects of lighting – those that are intended to elicit a more visceral response - including various ways to enhance the natural form of a subject with light, shadow and color and how to create an aesthetically pleasing composition. We'll also consider ways to better delineate between the foreground and background in the acting areas.

Each of these issues involves the selection of color and diffusion material – color to correct the color temperature and tone the lights, and diffusion material to blend and control the quality of light. Our lighting plot is not complete until we decide which colors and diffusion material to use in which lights and when to use them.

VISIBILITY AND AESTHETICS

Earlier in this book, we defined lighting design as the process of using light to shape the visual environment in order to achieve a stated objective or set of objectives. In this part of the book, we will distinguish between lighting for visibility and lighting for aesthetics.

The primary purpose of most lighting designs is to assist in visibility, whether it's for a live audience, one or more cameras, or both. But if that was the only the only objective, then it might suffice to just leave the house lights on. The key ingredient that's missing from the "house lights scenario" is the composition of a visually pleasing picture which reveals the subject, controls the contrast in the picture, and evokes an emotional response from the viewer. So we can say that the secondary purpose of a lighting design is to compose a variety of aesthetically pleasing looks for a live audience, one or more cameras, or both.

The issue of aesthetics and quality of light is much more subjective than the subjects of our previous discussions. What is visually appealing to one person might be uninspiring or ineffective to another. But there are certain approaches that can provide us with a starting point for creating an aesthetically pleasing composition. And then there are certain universal objectives we can strive to achieve in order to produce the best possible outcome. We might, for example, want to flatter the subject by bringing out highlights and softening wrinkles, defining contours with light and shadow – sometimes with soft shadows and at times with hard shadows - accentuate the form and create depth and separation between the subject and the background. We also want to create a colorful background or series of backgrounds that compliment and enhance the production. That's where the methodical approach comes in. Production values and aesthetics may vary according to the type of service; the carefully crafted look of a pastor during a traditional church service – making them look more intelligent, more engaging, and more influential – is completely different than crafting the look of a contemporary service with a praise and worship band. But the artistic value of a service is just as important in a traditional service as in a contemporary service. In either case, the quality of light will have a tremendous influence on the look and feel of the service.

The tools we use to accomplish our goals typically include lights with a limited palette of available colors from disparate sources with different hues, saturations and intensities. Our job is to creatively apply these tools to the problem at hand, and do so in an original way and an aesthetically pleasing way very quickly and efficiently. In short, we must use the lighting rig to address a variety of issues from the physical to the psychological.

Concepts:
The primary purpose of most lighting design is to assist in visibility for a live audience, one or more cameras, or both. The secondary purpose of lighting design is to compose a variety of aesthetically pleasing looks for a live audience, one or more cameras, or both.

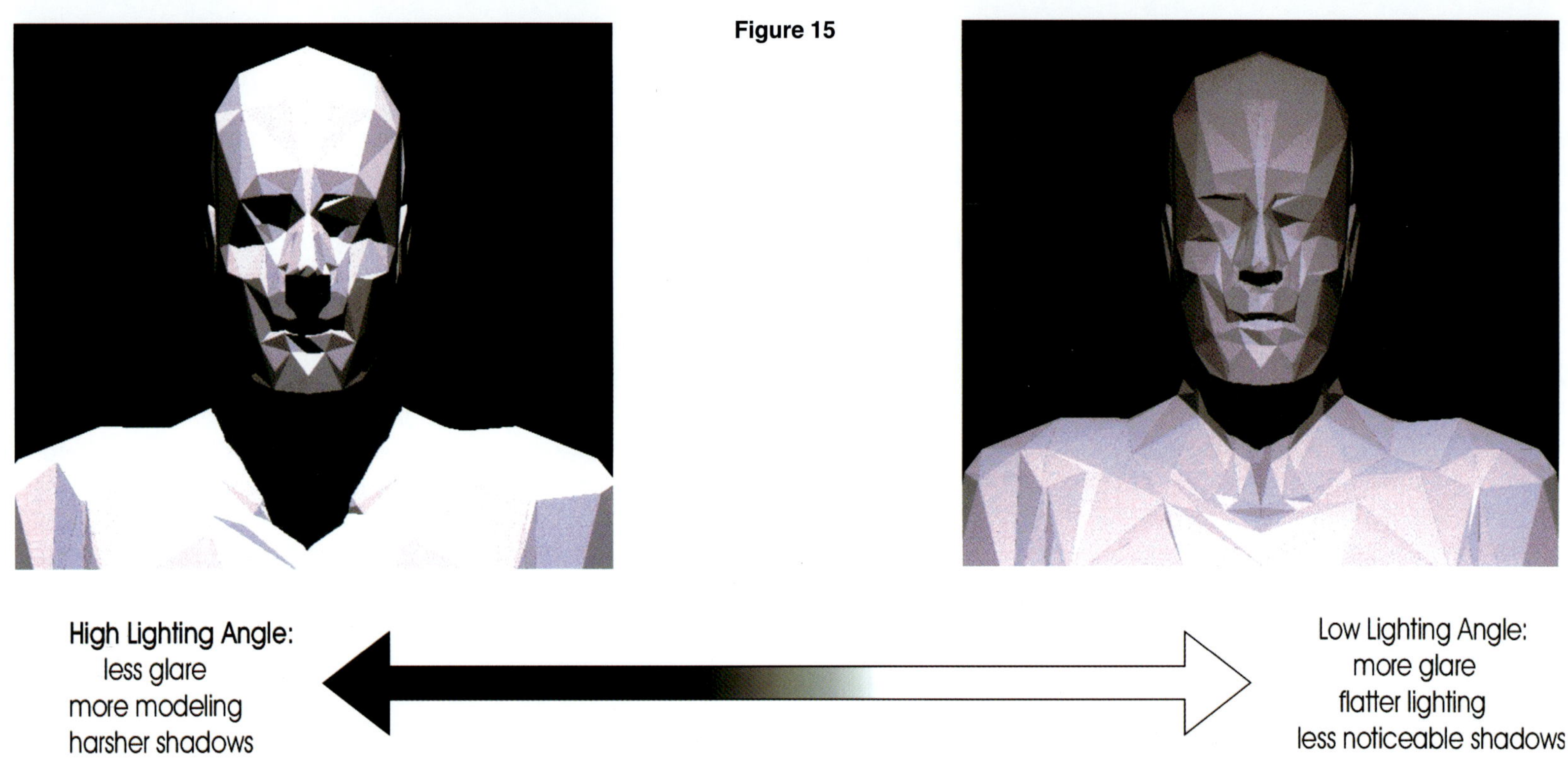

Figure 15 - Example of design choice and the associated compromise. There are many design choices to be made in a typical lighting design, each of which is a balance between competing outcomes.

THE DESIGNER'S MATRIX

The choices facing the lighting designer in any situation are many, and each decision influences a delicate balance in the final outcome of the product. Most every design is a series of choices we make with a compromise between two diametrically opposed outcomes. For example, we want our key light to light our subject without producing stark shadows in the eye sockets, under the nose, and under the jowls. We could place our key light at a low angle to accomplish this, but we know from the first part of this book that lighting angles below 45 degrees not only produce less severe shadows on the face, but they also produce more glare for the subject and a flat lighting look. Since one of our goals is to model the subject so that the audience gets a sense of the dimensions of the subject, including the contours of the subject and the set, then flat lighting will not help us accomplish these goals. And for practical reasons, we don't want the subject to suffer from the intense glare produced by very low lighting angles. Therefore, we might find that keeping the vertical angle of the key light at about 45 degrees is a good compromise; it decreases the glare while helping to model the subject with slightly more noticeable shadows, but not so much that it becomes distorted, surreal, or a distraction. This is only one example of the tradeoffs involved in making design decisions. There are many more.

Figure 16

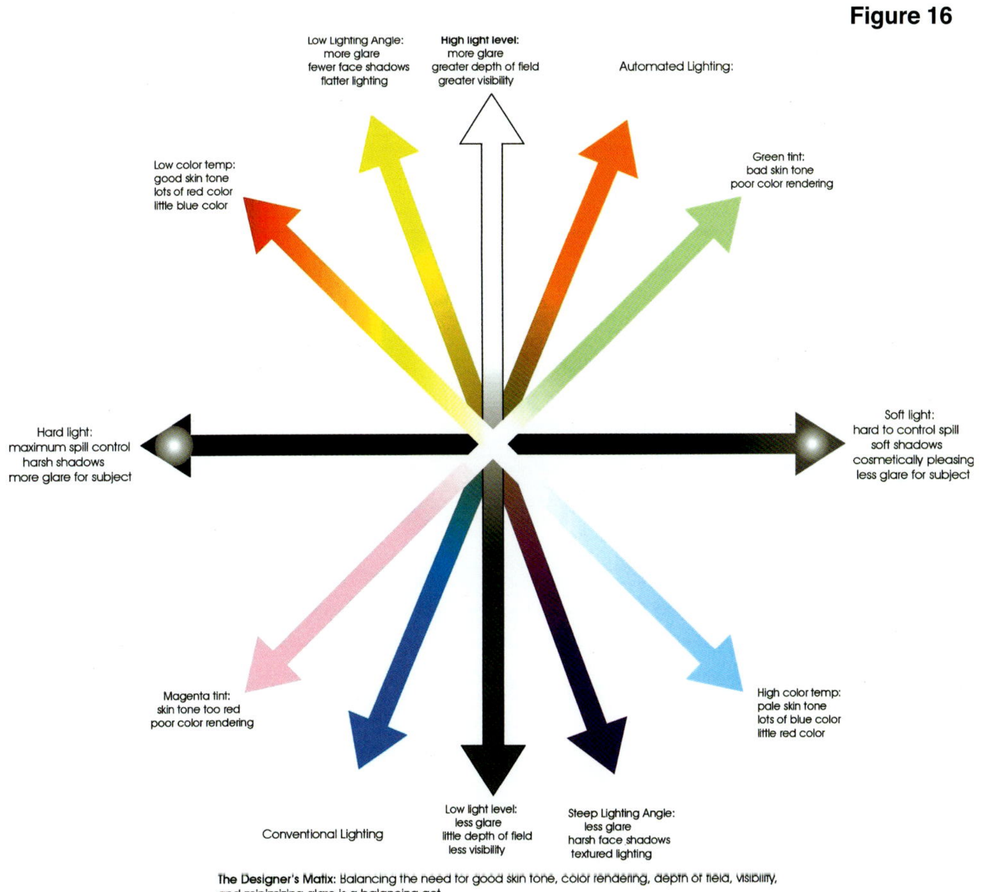

Concepts:

- Most every design decision comes with a compromise between two diametrically opposed outcomes.
- As a designer, it is our job to decide which options to take and when to take them.
- Each situation calls for a unique set of design choices based on the desired outcome.

Figure 16 - Design Choices Matrix. Every design choice is a compromise between two diametrically opposed options.

In every aspect of lighting design there are choices which affect the outcome – the type of lamp source, the color temperature, the amount of diffusion, the illuminance, etc. Understanding each of these choices and how they affect the final outcome helps us to decide which compromises are acceptable and which are not in order to make the best decisions for the application. There are many approaches to lighting design and no single approach works 100% of the time. But awareness of these issues is the precursor to developing an eye for recognizing and resolving them. With a little experience and a sharpened eye, all of these issues can be understood and resolved in the best possible way.

Figure 17

SCULPTING AND PAINTING WITH LIGHT

In some ways, using light is a similar to sculpting stone or painting a canvass. A sculptor draws form out of a block of stone by chipping away at the stone and a painter creates the illusion of depth by "massing" or modeling the canvass with various tints and shades of color. But a lighting designer draws form out of 3D space by emphasizing the contrast between light and dark and creating a relief of shadow and light. It is only by this contrast that the audience can distinguish form, shape and definition.

Leonardo da Vinci was one of the first artists to recognize the importance of emphasizing shadow to paint a compelling picture. "Shadows have their boundaries at certain determinable points," he said. "He who is ignorant of these will produce work without relief; and the relief is the summit and the soul of painting." Da Vinci was the originator of what is known as chiaroscuro – the use of contrast between light and dark for dramatic emphasis.

Before da Vinci, artists didn't understand how to effectively use shadows so they emphasized light instead, virtually ignoring shadows. That's not an uncommon approach in lighting – using more light instead of sculpting with shadow by selectively removing light. We are, after all, lighting designers and not shadow designers. And as the saying goes, if the only tool you have is a hammer, pretty soon everything starts looking like a nail. But light is not the only tool of a lighting designer. If we focus more on creating contrasts, then we can fully realize the tools at our disposal, i.e., light and shadow. And with those tools alone we can create more compelling art, just as da Vinci did with the Mona Lisa and The Last Supper.

Figure 17 - Leonardo da Vinci was the first painter to emphasize the importance of shadows in creating the illusion of depth on a two dimensional surface. Notice the depth and softness of the shadows in the Mona Lisa.

The mark of a good lighting designer is one who uses light and shadow to accentuate the form and dimension of a subject. By using backlight we can accentuate the outline of a subject and by using fill light we can control the amount and quality of the shadows and contours of the subject in much the same way that a painter masses or models a canvass.

QUALITY OF LIGHT

Have you ever noticed the difference in the quality of sunlight during different times of the day? In the morning when the sun is low in the sky, the light is a bit softer and the orange hues lower the color temperature and render a warm canvass across the landscape. The color temperature is lower because the light is traveling through the earth's atmosphere at a low angle, scattering it slightly and altering its intensity and color. As the sun rises higher in the sky it becomes more directional, more intense, and it produces sharper shadows as well as having a higher color temperature. When it reaches its zenith the light is at its peak intensity and color temperature and it is most directional because it is traveling through the least amount of atmosphere.

When the sky is overcast, the clouds scatter the light, producing less directional light and softer shadows. Many photographers prefer overcast days to clear sunny days because the quality of light is more suited for portrait photography. By the same token, moonlight is much softer light than sunlight because sunlight is direct while moonlight is reflected light. When the moon reflects the light of the sun it scatters it and it becomes less directional.

Figure 18

Figure 18 - Direct versus indirect light. Moonlight is softer because it's more scattered than direct sunlight.

These are examples of how the quality of light can vary and alter our perception of the same subject. Claude Monet (1840-1926), a French impressionist painter, was a keen observer of the quality of light. He used to rise early in the morning and begin painting outdoors as the sun was creeping above the horizon. Every half hour, as the light changed, he would begin a new painting, reflecting the changes in the series of paintings of the same subject.

We can't control the weather or the time of day, but as lighting designers we can control the quality of light by introducing diffusion to control the softness of light, gels to alter the color temperature, and dimmers to control the intensity of the light. In addition, we can control the atmosphere by using set pieces, projection surfaces, soft goods, color wash, aerial beams and pattern projection to compose a cohesive design.

Figure 19 - French impressionist Claude Monet painted a series showing a haystack under different lighting conditions, illustrating how the quality of light can change a subject.

Figure 20

Figure 20 - Hard light (left) versus soft light (right). Hard light is directional, and produces well defined shadows with sharp edges that tend to distort the picture. Soft light produces more natural looking soft shadows.

Concepts:

- The mark of a good lighting designer is one who uses light and dark to accentuate and bring out the form and dimension of a subject.
- The quality of light can completely change our perception of a subject.

Words to Know

- Chiaroscuro – the use of bold contrast between light and dark for dramatic emphasis

HARD LIGHT AND SOFT LIGHT

One of the many design choices a lighting designer must make is when and where to use hard (directional) light, soft (scattered) light, or something in between. As with most every other design choice, there are trade offs and consequences that come with each of these decisions.

Hard light, or very directional light, is easier to control; it conforms to shutter cuts and it can be controlled with barn doors. This is especially important when there are video screens on the set; if you ever want to see a video director on the verge of a nervous breakdown, try throwing some light onto the video screen.

But directional light also tends to produce sharp, well-defined shadows. It accentuates textures and shows most every blemish and contour on the subject. This can be desirable or undesirable, depending on the application – are we lighting the Marlboro Man or are we lighting Marilyn Monroe? Directional lighting can reveal detail in a set piece or the texture of a wall or surface but it can also sharpen and reveal details that are best left obscured.

Soft light, or diffuse light, is harder to control because it's more scattered by its nature and it doesn't conform well to shutter cuts. But depending on the amount of diffusion, it can be controlled to some extent with barn doors and flags. The beauty of soft light is that it tends to produce very soft shadows that create nice, smooth transitions between light and dark. Soft light is flattering to subjects because it obscures age line, blemishes, and wrinkles, and no one wants to look wrinkled.

DIFFUSION

The hardness or softness of light can be controlled by the choice of luminaire and the use of diffusion. The most directional light is produced by a point source. Focusable luminaires, like a profile spot or ERS fixture, with a compact lamp source are examples of such a light. Softer light is produced by a linear or very large source. A de-focused ERS with diffusion material in front of it or a Fresnel fixture are two examples of a soft source.

Adding diffusion material allows you to control the amount of diffusion over and above the softness of the source. In effect, it acts to make the source of light bigger. The farther from the lamp the diffusion is placed, the more pronounced the effect of softening the light. Putting a diffusion gel directly onto the lens of an ERS does little more than widen the beam. But placing it several inches in front of the lens softens the edges of the beam and produces softer shadows.

In addition to, or as a result of scattering the light, diffusion can also alter the field, beam, intensity and the color temperature. Some diffusion material is designed to soften the edge of the beam while maintaining the original beam shape, some will increase the beam size and some will elongate the beam in one direction. All diffusion decreases the efficiency of a luminaire because some of the light is absorbed by the diffusion material – the heavier the diffusion the greater the light loss. All of these characteristics of diffusion material should be taken into consideration in the design process when selecting and using them.

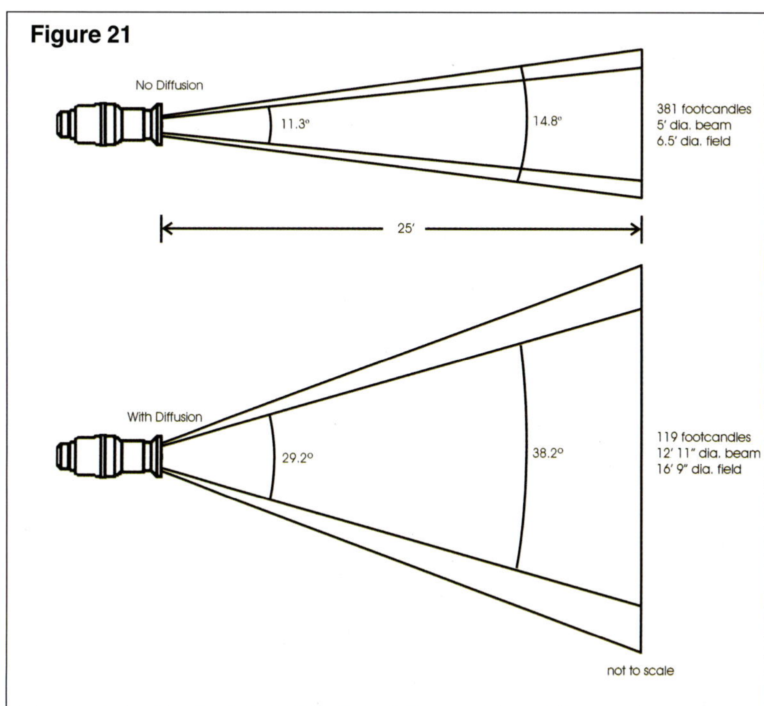

Figure 21 - Adding heavy diffusion reduces the illuminance and increases the size of the beam and field.

For example, Roscolux 116 Tough White Diffusion is a heavy diffusion with the following characteristics:

- **Transmission: 31.25%**
- **F-stop change: 1 2/3**
- **Color temperature drop from 3200K: –150K**
- **% increase in beam angle: +258%**

Concepts:

- Hard light, or highly directional light, produces hard shadows, accentuates details and conforms to beam control with shutters and barn doors.
- Soft light, or scattered light, produces soft shadows and obscured details, but it is harder to control with shutters and barn doors.

Words to Know

- Directional light – non-scattered light.
- Diffuse light – scattered light.

Suppose we are using an ETC Source Four with a 14 degrees lens and an HPL 575/115X lamp, and we want to use it for fill light at a throw of 30 feet. Without diffusion, the illumination at that throw distance is 381 footcandles, the beam diameter is 5 feet, and the field diameter is 6.5 feet. When we add a single sheet of Roscolux 116, then the illumination drops to 119 footcandles, the beam diameter widens to 12' 11" and the field diameter widens to 16' 9".

EXPOSURE VALUES

There is a wide variety of diffusion material available from Apollo, GAM, Lee and Rosco, ranging from very light, almost imperceptible diffusion to very heavy diffusion. Some gel manufacturers include quantitative information about each type of diffusion material including the transmission (the amount of incident light that passes through the material) and how it affects the f-stop or exposure value on a camera. Each time the light reaching the camera is cut in half it represents a full f-stop, assuming the aperture setting remains unchanged. For example, if adding diffusion to a luminaire reduces the amount of light reaching the camera by 50%, then the exposure value is cut in half. To keep the exposure value the same, the camera should be adjusted a full stop to compensate. If the same diffusion material is doubled, then the light reaching the camera will be cut by 75% (half of half is 25%) and the camera should be adjusted two full camera stops.

Not all manufacturers of diffusion material include information about f-stops or transmission, but usually those whose products are commonly used in the motion picture industry where exact light measurements are more critical, do. Some diffusion material also affects the color temperature, but again, many of the manufacturers do not quantify the amount of the color temperature shift. Most of them only give some written description of the amount of diffusion, transmission and color temperature shift introduced by each type of diffusion material. In addition, much of the information manufacturers provide about their diffusion material is based on placing the material either at the source, as in the color gel frame slot, or at some distance from the source as in placing it on a C-stand. The results vary quite a bit between these two positions. It's best to experiment and find what works best for your application. But don't assume that because you see the edge of the beam soften that the shadows on the face will also soften. Look closely and verify the results for yourself because they might surprise you.

DEGREES OF DIFFUSION

Diffusion material can be classified according to the amount of diffusion it provides, how it affects the beam edge, and how it affects the beam shape. The amount of diffusion is related to the transmission – the heavier the diffusion the lower the transmission. In general terms, the amount of diffusion can be classified as:

- **Light diffusion (transmission approximately 99% ~ 60%)**
- **Medium diffusion (transmission approximately 65% ~ 30%)**
- **Heavy diffusion (transmission approximately 35% ~ 1%)**

The amount of diffusion you use depends on the application and the requirements of the project. When you use diffusion with an ellipsoidal reflector spotlight (ERS) and put it in the gel holder, it tends to be less effective than mounting large sheets of it on a C-stand and placing it farther away from the light source. But this method, which is popular in film and studio photography, is impractical with a live audience because it blocks sight lines. The closer to the lamp source the diffusion material is placed, the less effective it is for softening shadows. For this reason, light and medium diffusion does little to soften face shadows, though they will certainly soften the beam edge and widen the field.

Heavy diffusion is very effective soft light that softens shadows, obscures line, wrinkles and blemishes. It can make the task of lighting for video a bit easier in that it reduces the contrast in the details of a subject, making for a softer picture and a younger-looking subject. A good example can be seen on the morning news show on CNN called "Robin & Company."

Figure 22 - Robin Meade, the host of CNN's "Robin & Company" is portrayed in very soft light, which is very flattering to the subject.

Soft light also tends to wrap around the subject because it is so scattered. Therefore, it works well as side light or backlight.

Heavily diffused light is also very flat lighting with little character. Too much diffusion makes the subject look two-dimensional. In addition to softening age lines and wrinkles, it also obscures other information about the texture and form of the subject. For example, it renders folds of cloth indistinguishable and eliminates detail and depth. It does not work well in instances where the subject should be portrayed as weathered or "experienced."

In video production, soft boxes are often used for key light. A soft box is a light source with a shroud and a large diffusion surface that produces soft light. Because they are so large, they block lines of sight and are not practical for use in houses of worship where the congregation needs to be able to see the platform.

Since you lose some ability to control the direction and spill with diffusion, it is a good idea to use it cautiously. You might, for example, use it in all the side lights and not in the front light. That way, you can soften the shadows created by the side light and still retain control of the spill on the lights that are most likely to affect the scenery – the front lights.

Concepts:

- Adding diffusion material to a luminaire allows you to control the softness or hardness of the light.
- Diffusion can alter the intensity, size, shape and color temperature of a light.
- All diffusion reduces the efficiency of a source.
- Each time the light intensity is halved, the f-stop should be increased by one f-stop in order to compensate.
- The closer to the light source diffusion is placed, the less effect is has on softening shadows.
- Soft light tends to wrap around a subject.
- Heavily diffused light tends to produce flat lighting.

Words to Know

- F-stop – an exposure value on a camera that corresponds to a doubling or halving of the light intensity.

COLOR TEMPERATURE

In addition to using diffusion, another design decision that must be made is to match all the sources to a dominant color temperature. If the majority of the lights are incandescent, then their natural color temperature at full intensity will be between about 2900K and 3200K, depending on the type of lamp with which they are fitted. If the majority of lights have discharge sources, then the correlated color temperature could be anywhere from about 5600K to 6800K or higher. As the designer, we should know what type of lamp is being used and what color temperature it is.

Whether we're using incandescent lamps or discharge lamps, all of the sources should be matched so that they look the same, to the extent possible, on camera as well as to the naked eye. This is a simple matter of using color correction gels, or, in the case of automated lights, using their variable color correction feature, if they are so equipped. Some automated lights have a gradient density filter with a thin-film optical coating that gradually increases or decreases the color temperature. If you happen to be using lights that don't have this feature, then using a cut from a color correction gel taped over the exit lens with gaff tape can accomplish the task.

Color temperature correction gels generally come in two varieties; correct to orange (CTO) and correct to blue (CTB). A CTO filter lowers the color temperature of a source and a CTB filter raises the color temperature of a source. These filters are generally available in steps of ⅛, ¼, ½, ¾ and full CTO or CTB.

MIRED SHIFTS

How much does a full CTO or CTB shift the color temperature? It depends on the color temperature that you're starting with. For that reason it is more accurate to measure the shift introduced by a color correction filter in terms of microreciprocal degrees or "mireds." A mired is 1,000,000 divided by the color temperature.

M (mireds) = 1,000,000 ÷ color temperature (K)

So we can say, for example, that 5500K is the same as 182 mireds (1,000,000 ÷ 5500 ~ 182).

Working with color correction filters is simplified using mireds because they are additive. By converting a color temperature to its mired equivalent, we can add the effect of the filter in mireds to arrive at the final color temperature. For example, suppose a CTO filter changes a 6500K source to 3200K. Let's examine the change in terms of mireds.

6500K = 153.9 mireds
3200K = 312.5 mireds
Change in color temperature = - 3300K
Mired shift = +158.6

Now suppose we use the same CTO filter with a source that is starting at 5500K. Remember, the filter produces a mired shift of +158.6. Therefore:

5500K = 181.8
Mired shift = +158.6

Final mired value = 181.8 + 158.6
= 340.4 mireds

340.4 mireds = 1,000,000 ÷
final color temperature

Final color temperature = 2937.6K

Difference in color temperature = 2562.4K

As we can see, when we started with a color temperature of 6500K, the CTO shifted the source by 3300K, but when we started with a color temperature of 5500K, the same filter only shifted the source by 2562.4K. The constant, however, is the mired shift, which is +158.6 in both cases. A filter with a positive mired shift lowers the color temperature and one with a negative mired shift raises the color temperature.

It is important to understand mireds because using them is the only accurate way to figure out which gel you need to use to correct a particular source. Most every color correction filter gives you the mired shift associated with it.

Figure 24

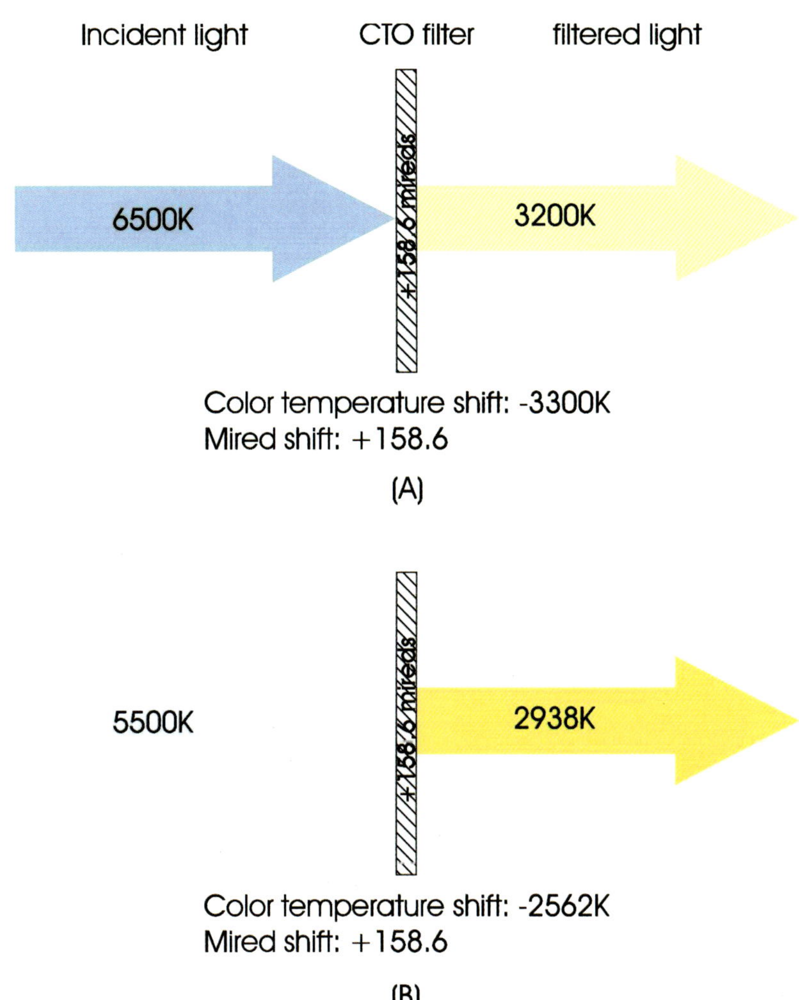

Figure 24 - A color correction filter shifts color temperature by different amounts depending on the starting color temperature. The mireds shift, however, is the same in each case.

MATCHING SOURCES

If an event is only for the benefit of a live audience, then matching the color temperature of all the sources is not as critical as it is when video is involved because the human eye is more forgiving than is a camera. If the event is to be broadcast, taped, or shown on video for image-magnification, then it's very important that all of the light sources used on the subjects have matching color temperatures. Otherwise, a subject could be rendered on video with a very different skin tone, depending on which light is being used.

The video camera can be "white balanced" to any color temperature, so is it better to balance to daylight or is it better to balance to tungsten? What's more important is that all the sources are matched to the same color temperature, especially those that will be lighting the subject or subjects. After that, it's up for debate whether one color temperature is better or preferable to another. Some people like to use HMIs and balance everything to daylight, some like to balance to tungsten because it's a warmer color that might better lend itself to flattering skin tones. Still others like to balance in between daylight and tungsten as a compromise. Just remember that when you dim incandescent lights they drop in color temperature, so balance the cameras with the key light set to the proper level.

Concepts:

- Lamp sources should be matched in color temperature so that they look the same, to the extent possible, on camera as well as to the naked eye.
- A CTO filter lowers the color temperature of a source and a CTB filter raises the color temperature of a source.
- A mired is 1,000,000 divided by the color temperature. (Mired Shift = 1,000,000 ÷ color temperature (K))
- Mireds are additive.
- A positive mired shift lowers the color temperature of a light source and a negative mired shift raises the color temperature of a light source.

Words to Know

- CTO – correct to orange.
- CTB – correct to blue.
- Mireds – microreciprocal degrees

"I myself do nothing. The Holy Spirit accomplishes all through me."
— William Blake

Chapter 7

COLOR WASH

Adding colored lighting, even if it's a small amount, is a very effective way to liven up a lighting composition. It can be used to wash large surface areas such as a light colored backdrop or to add an accent here and there, such as on a series of white columns. There are also times when it's appropriate to wash the entire platform with color, such as when a praise and worship band is playing.

There are many ways to create a good color wash. The simplest is to use PAR cans with colored gels. To get more utility from them we can also add a color scroller to each PAR can. That will allow us to remotely select from a choice of up to 32 different colors on each PAR can, or in the case of a color mixing scroller, many more colors. Alternatively, we could use automated color wash fixtures or automated profile spot fixtures to remotely change the focus and color of each instrument. These luminaires can be relatively expensive, but there are a number of color changing fixtures that don't pan and tilt; they cost somewhere between a PAR can with a scroller and an automated luminaire. All of these are effective ways of creating a color wash.

We should consider designing color wash into your lighting system with something other than automated lights or in addition to automated lights. That's because, if the budget needs to be cut, the first thing to go is often the automated lighting. If we don't have an alternative for providing a color wash, then we will be left with nothing but no-color white light. That happened to me a couple of times before I realized the importance of specifying more than one type of color wash fixture.

Once we decide where to put our color wash fixtures, then we need to decide which colors to use in them. That's where an understanding of color theory will serve us well. Most color theory comes from the art world, though a painter uses subtractive color while the lighting designer uses additive color.

SELECTING COLOR

One of the most important design decisions is choosing colors for our color wash. Sometimes there are very specific color requirements, such as the colors of a logo or certain theme colors such as Christmas or the Fourth of July. Barring those circumstances, our choice of colors should reflect the needs of the production over our personal favorites. The colors we use have a major influence on the look of the design and if we understand basic concepts of color it can help us create intelligent and effective designs.

Some people believe that form affects people's intellect and color affects people's emotions. It is the emotional component that we want to address by choosing certain colors or color combinations. Color can be very subjective and different people may have different reactions to the same colors. On the other hand, there are very specific ways that we can use color to create strong contrasts, harmony and disharmony.

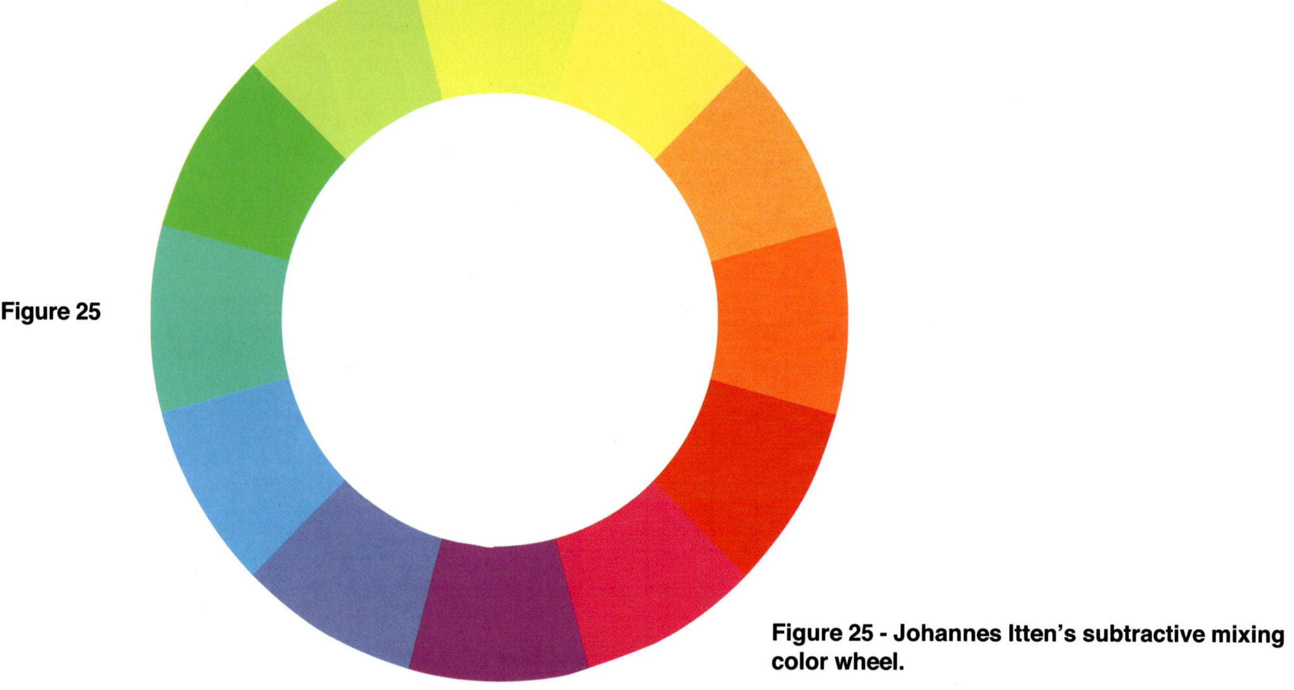

Figure 25

Figure 25 - Johannes Itten's subtractive mixing color wheel.

COLOR THEORY

Most modern color theory is based on the color wheel and the way colors interact with each other. The first color wheel was devised by Sir Isaac Newton in the 1600s when he discovered that sunlight was made up of a spectrum of colors. Since then, several contributions have been made to the study of color theory by such people as Johann Wolfgang von Goethe, Michel Chevreul, Johannes Itten, and Josef Albers.

THE COLOR WHEEL

After several modifications to the original color wheel, Johannes Itten devised a color wheel based on the work of Chevreul and others. He used it to teach art classes at Bauhaus in the early 1900s and he wrote about it in his classic book on color called "The Art of Color." It looks like that shown in **Figure 25.**

Notice that the color wheel is arranged around the three equally spaced primaries – red, blue, and yellow. Exactly midway between each primary is one of the secondary colors – green, orange, and purple, and between each secondary color is a tertiary color – blue-green, green-yellow, yellow-orange, orange-red, red-purple, and purple-blue. This is the color wheel that most painters use today. With a little modification to distinguish between how a painter uses color and how a lighting designer uses color, we can make good use of the color wheel. We'll discuss more about that later.

ITTEN'S SEVEN CONTRASTS

Johannes Itten recognized seven ways of creating contrast with color, and these contrasts can help us with lighting design as much as they help a painter design a canvass. The seven contrasts are:

Figure 26

- **Contrast of saturation** – the contrast between two colors of the same hue but with different levels of saturation.
- **Contrast of light and dark** – the contrast between light and dark, including that of light and shadow.
- **Contrast of proportion** – the contrast between two or more colors covering greater or lesser areas, e.g., 75% green contrasted with 25% red.
- **Contrast of complements** – the contrast between complementary colors such as purple/yellow or blue/orange.
- **Simultaneous contrast** – the contrast between two colors that are so strongly opposite that they create the illusion of movement or vibration.
- **Contrast of hue** – the contrast between two colors of different hue.
- **Contrast of warm and cool** – the contrast between warm colors and cool colors.

Figure 26 - Itten's contrasts: (A) Contrast of saturation; (B) Contrast of light and dark; (C) Contrast of proportion; (D) Contrast of complements; (E) Simultaneous contrast; (F) Contrast of hue; (G) Contrast of warm and cool.

Concepts:

- Color, and people's reaction to color, is subjective.
- Color theory is based on the color wheel and how colors interact with each other.
- Sir Isaac Newton discovered that white light is composed of the spectrum of colors.
- Johannes Itten recognized that there are seven types of color contrast: contrast of saturation, contrast of light and dark, contrast of proportion, contrast of complements, simultaneous contrast, contrast of hues, and contrast of warm and cool.

Words to Know

- Primary – first in a hierarchy.
- Secondary – second in a hierarchy.
- Tertiary – third in a hierarchy.

COLORS IN LIGHTING DESIGN

We can use the principles of color theory developed by artists such as Itten and Albers as a basis for creating contrast and harmony in our lighting design. Since color harmony is, for the most part, subjective rather than totally objective, we should keep in mind that color theory is simply a starting point and the needs and wants of the design are not to be superseded by a blind application of these principles.

PRIMARY COLORS

Itten's color wheel is based on the three primaries – red, blue, and yellow. But depending on the application, the primary colors can be either red, blue and green, or they can be red, blue and yellow. For an artist working with paint, it is important to be able to mix pure hues of primary color to create secondary colors. Therefore, such an artist considers red, blue and yellow to be the primaries because blue and yellow can be mixed together to produce green. However, an artist working with light who mixes blue and yellow will end up with white. To get yellow, the artist working with light must mix red and green.

The main difference between these two scenarios is that the painter is using subtractive color mixing while the lighting designer uses additive color mixing. When a painter puts pigment on a canvass, that pigment absorbs or subtracts every color in the spectrum except the color of the pigment. For example, yellow pigment subtracts all the blue and red and reflects yellow, which is what the eye sees. It's the same principle as a CMY color mixing system. The full-spectrum light that passes through a yellow filter in the CMY system becomes yellow because the blue light is blocked and the red and green light is passed (red + green = yellow). Or if a magenta filter in a CMY system is used instead, then the yellow light is blocked and the red and blue light is passed (red + blue = magenta). Now suppose we use both the yellow and the magenta filters – what color will result? The yellow filter passes red and green and the magenta filter passes red and blue, so the only color that passes through both filters is red, which is what our eye will see. That's how a subtractive color system works.

Figure 27

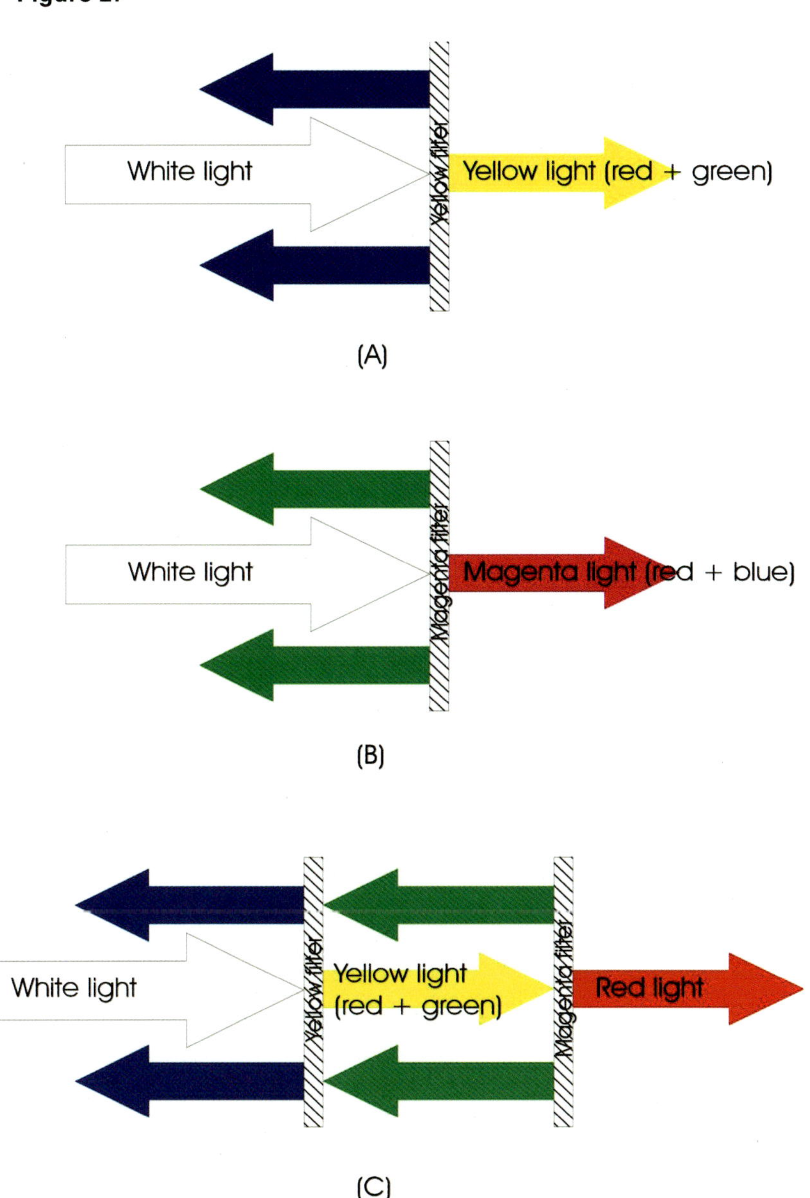

Figure 27 - A CMY color mixing system showing the subtractive method. (A) A yellow filter blocks blue and passes red and green, producing yellow light. (B) A magenta filter blocks green and passes red and blue, producing magenta light. (C) A yellow and magenta filter in series blocks blue and green and passes red light.

Figure 28

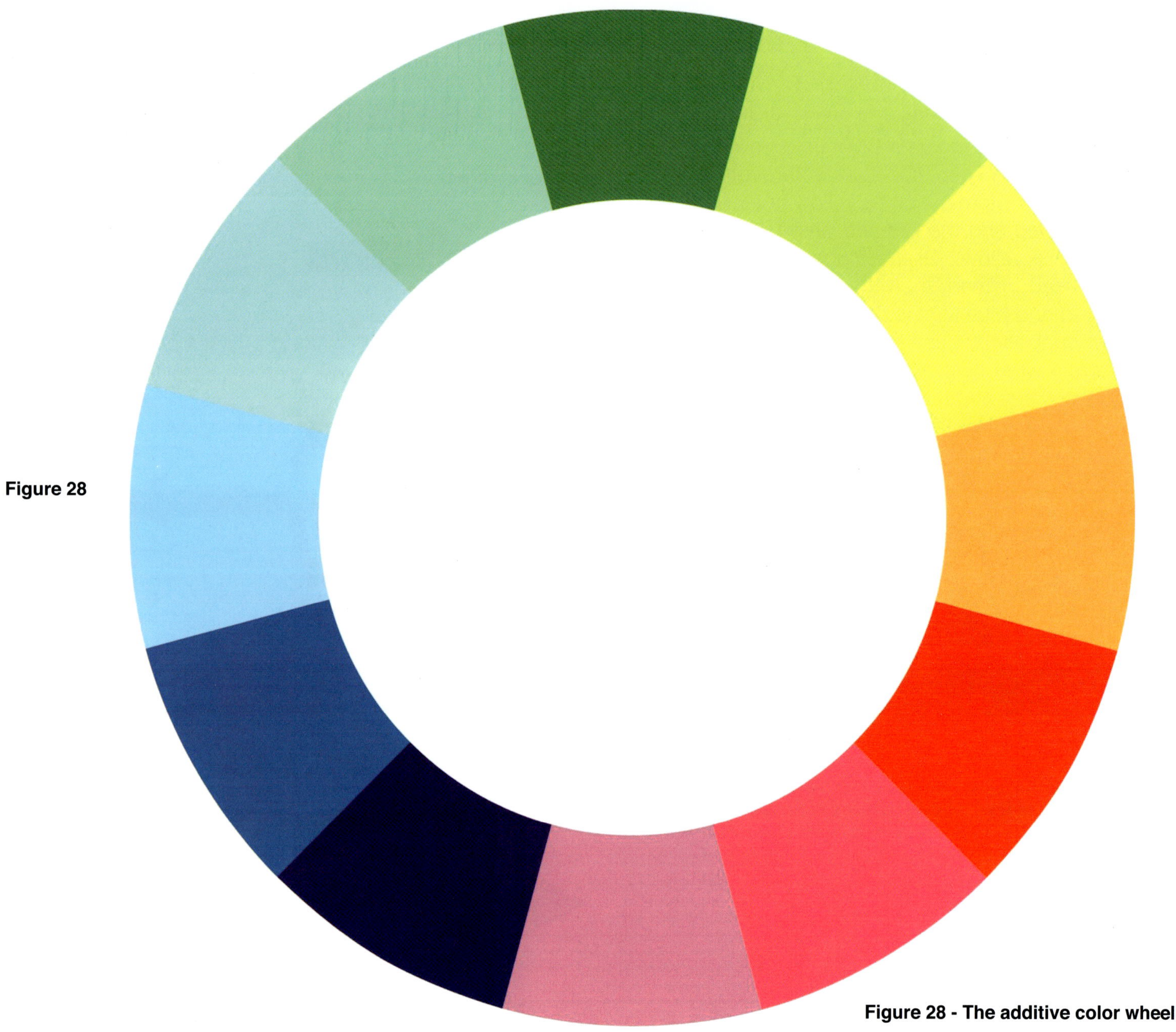

Figure 28 - The additive color wheel.

But a lighting designer is more concerned with additive color because the light emanating from a fixture is additive. When we mix red and green light it produces yellow. Therefore, we can recognize the difference between the additive primary colors – red, blue, and green – and the subtractive primary colors – red, blue, and yellow. With that in mind we can rearrange the color wheel to reflect our concern with additive primaries as follows.

SECONDARY AND TERTIARY COLORS

Secondary colors are those colors that can be obtained by mixing any two primary colors. These are: cyan (blue + green); magenta (red + blue); and yellow (red + green) and they are equidistant from each of the primary colors. Tertiary colors are those in between each pair of primary and secondary colors. These are: green-yellow; orange; red-magenta; indigo; blue-cyan; and green-blue.

Concepts:

- The additive primaries are red, blue, and green.
- The subtractive primaries are red, blue, and yellow.
- The additive secondary colors are cyan, magenta, and yellow.
- The additive tertiary colors are green-yellow; orange; red-magenta; indigo; blue-cyan; and green-blue.

Words to Know

- Additive – relating to the addition of.
- Subtractive – relating to the subtraction of.

Figure 29

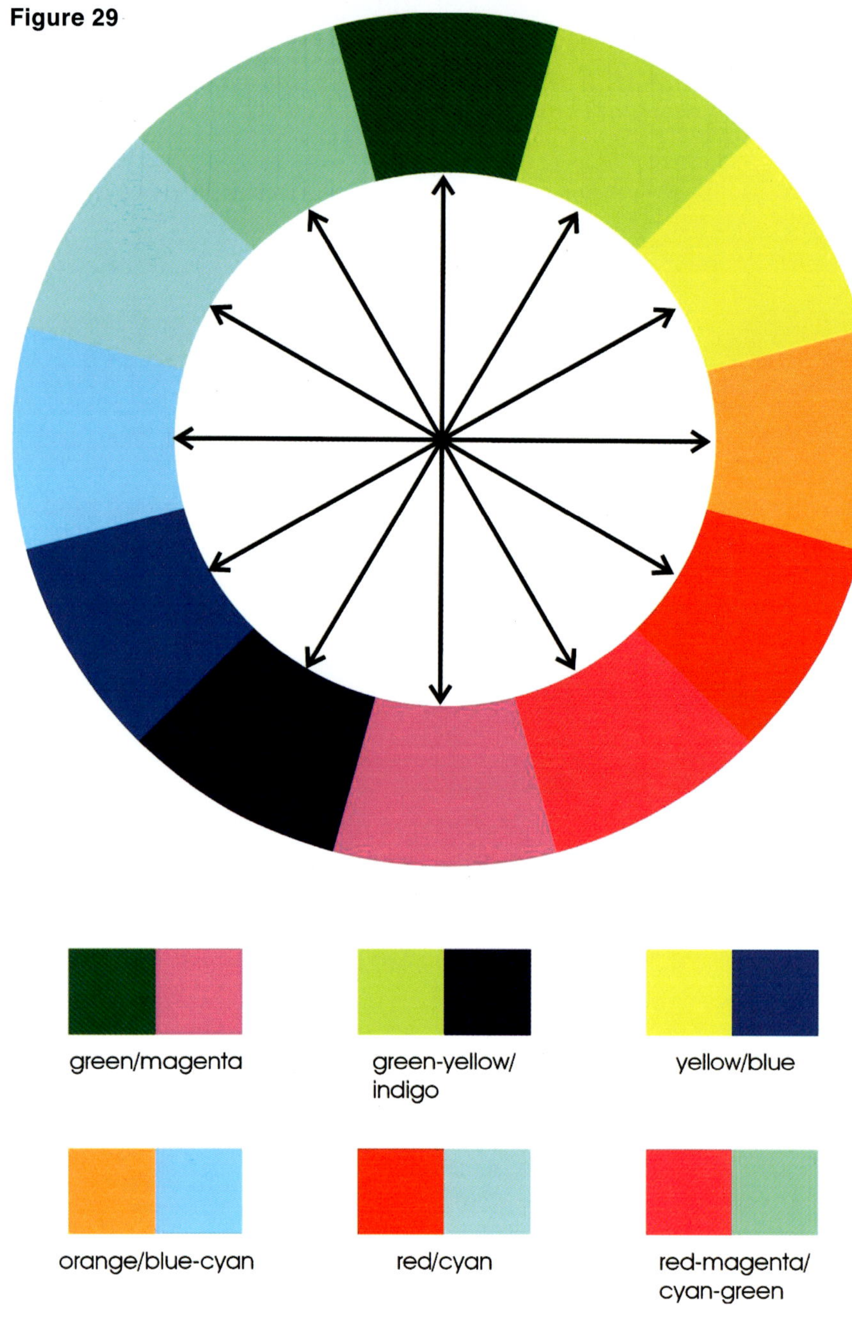

COMPLEMENTARY COLORS

Complementary colors are pairs of colors which, when added together, produce white light. For example, we know that mixing red, blue and green light makes white light. Since red mixed with blue makes magenta, then we can deduce that magenta and green are complementary colors.

The combination of the human eye and brain seeks color balance and harmony in visual composition much the same way the ear and brain seek resolution in musical composition. Complementary colors provide color harmony. They are easily found as opposite pairs on the color wheel. Rather than mixing them together, if we use them side-by-side, then we can create some interesting and useful color compositions.

Using our additive color wheel, we have six complementary color pairs that we can use as a basis or starting point for creating a lighting scene. They are:

- Magenta/green
- Indigo/green-yellow
- Blue/yellow
- Blue-cyan/ orange
- Cyan/red
- Cyan-green/red-magenta

Figure 29 - Complementary color pairs.

OTHER COLOR HARMONIES

Combining colors in complementary pairs is one example of a way to create harmony between colors. There are several other ways to accomplish similar effects. Some examples are outlined below.

SPLIT COMPLEMENTARY COLORS

One color plus the two colors on either side of its complementary color is a split complementary color combination. For example, green, indigo and red-magenta works together very well. There are twelve such combinations that we can derive from our color wheel.

Figure 30

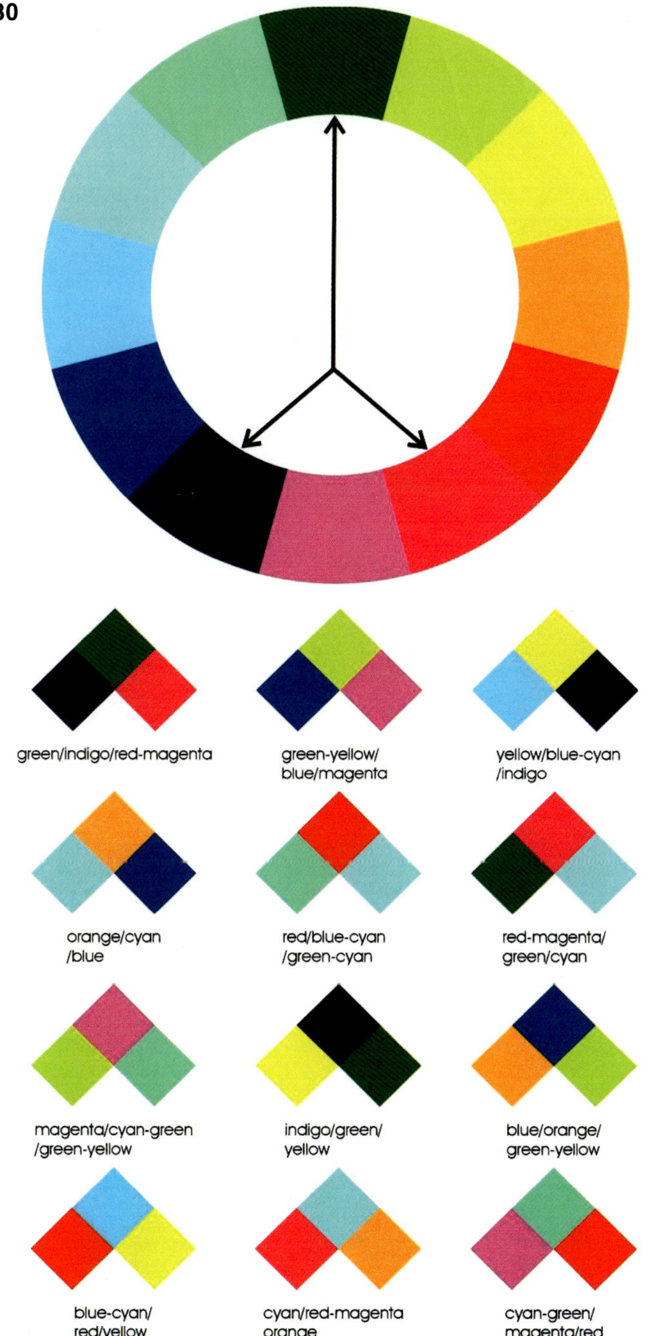

Figure 30 - Split complementary colors.

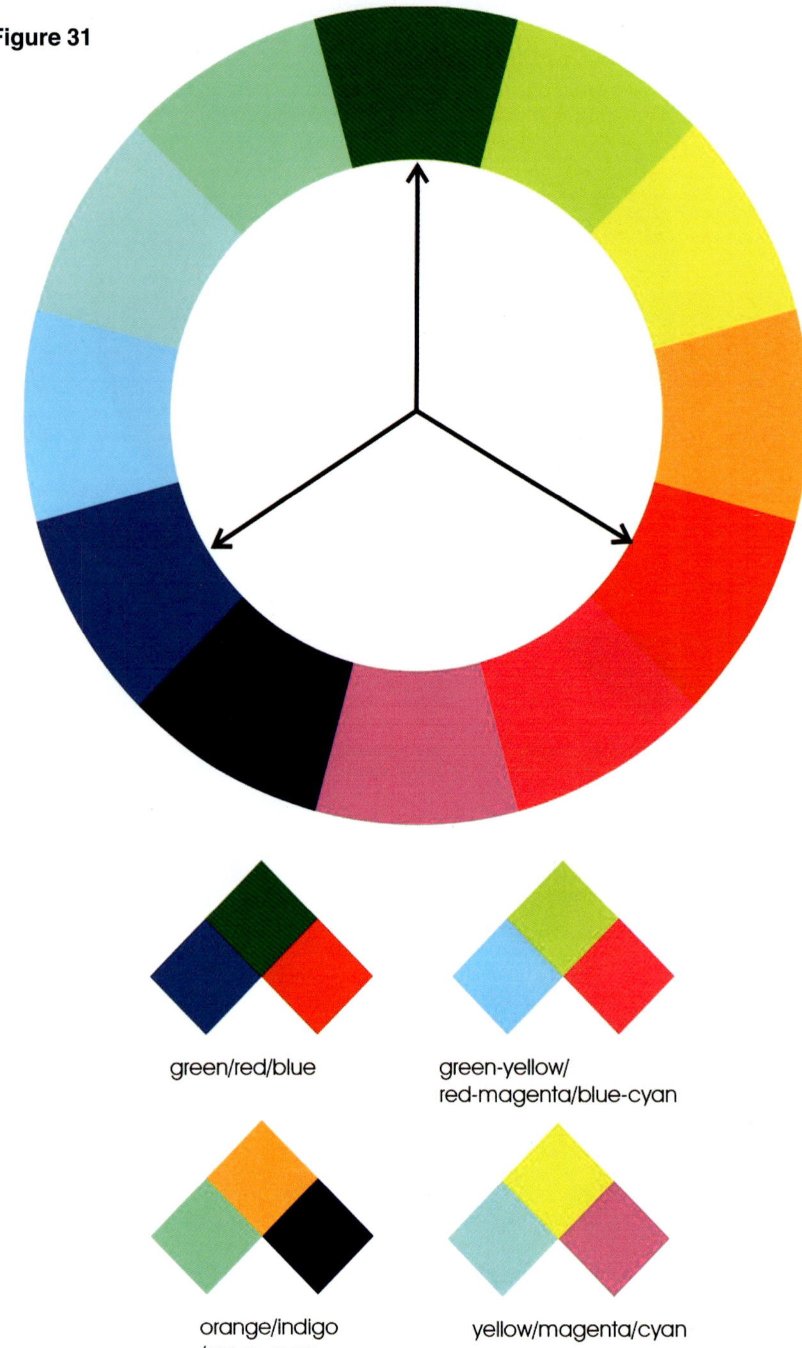

TRIADS

Three colors equidistant apart on the color wheel constitute a triad. Notice of the four possible triads, one uses all the primary colors, one uses all the secondary colors, and the last two use combinations of tertiary colors.

Figure 31 - Triads. Of the four possible three-color combinations of triads, one uses all the primaries, one uses all secondaries, and two use tertiary colors.

Figure 32

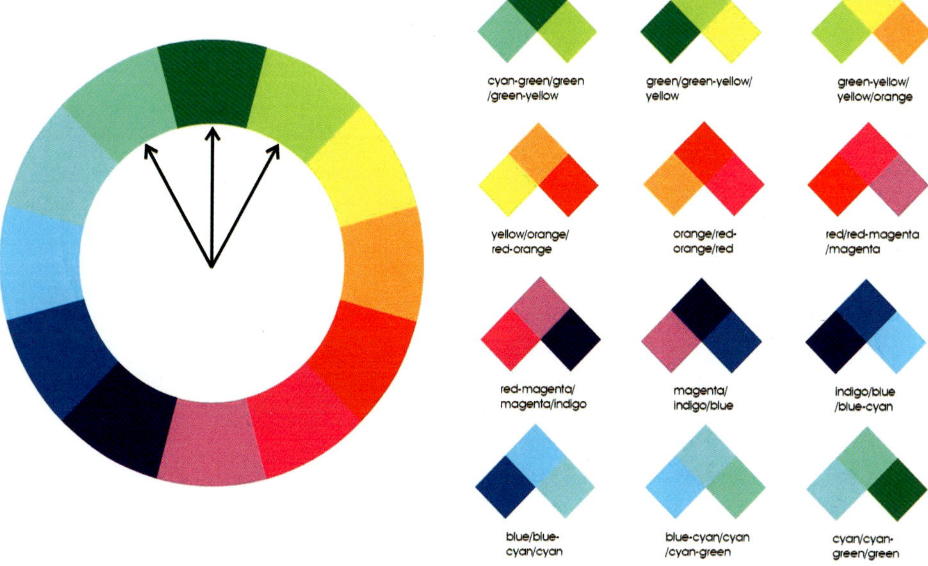

ANALOGOUS COLORS

Strong color combinations can be found by using analogous colors, or colors that are side-by-side in the color wheel. It can be a two-color combination such as blue/indigo, or a three-color combination such as blue/indigo/magenta. There are 12 two-color combinations and 12 three-color combinations in our color wheel.

Figure 32 - Analogous three-color (top) and two-color combinations.

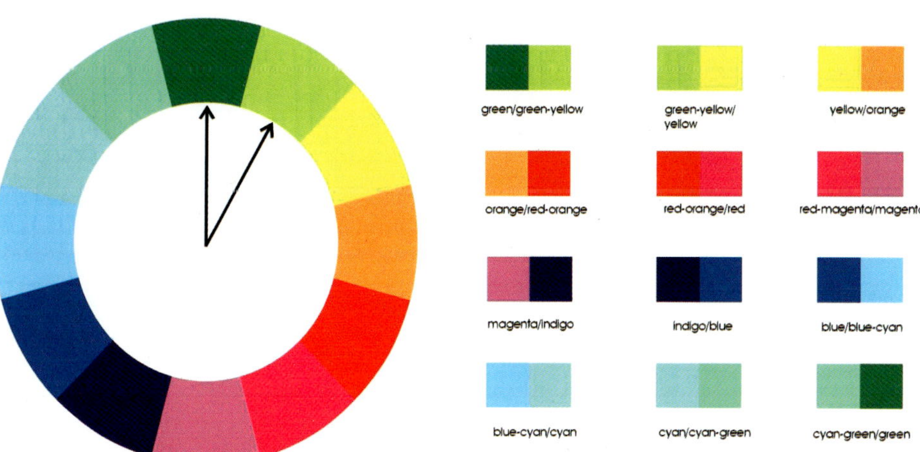

Figure 33

Figure 33 - White light can be combined with any single color to create effective contrast. (Artist: Big Daddy Weave; Lighting designers: Andrew Wakeman, Phil Gilbert, Richard Cadena; Production company: Maxx Productions)

White Light

Any color or combination of colors can be combined with white to expand the catalog of color combinations. In terms the seven types of contrast previously discussed, white can be used to create three of them: contrast of saturation, contrast of light and dark, and contrast of proportion. For example, white and any single color can take on the feel of a deeply saturated color contrasted with a completely washed out color. Or it can be used very effectively to create contrast with some well-placed shadows. Lastly, it can be used to change the proportion of a single-color wash to a wash with accents

SINGLE COLORS AND COLOR SYMBOLISM

A single color can be used as symbolism to very effectively create a strong association with a particular feel or emotion. A big uniform wash of a single color can be monotonous but we have the benefit of creating an interesting composition by introducing textures in the form of gobos, aerial beams (with sufficient haze or other interference medium) or set pieces such as soft goods or hard set pieces. Certain colors have a strong association with a particular emotion or subliminal suggestion. For example, when you think of passion, does the color purple come to mind? Other strong color associations include:

- **Red** – aggressive, dangerous, dynamic, energetic, strong, fire, blood, Coca-Cola, laser light, rock 'n' roll!
- **Green** – monster skin, alien skin, forest, trees, grass, money, envy, emeralds, St. Patrick's Day, Celtic culture
- **Blue** – cold, ice, melancholy, sky, IBM
- **Purple** – passion, mysticism, royalty
- **Yellow** – cowardice, sunshine
- **Orange** –sunset
- **White** – purity, clouds, snow, peace, surrender

Concepts:

- Complementary colors are pairs of colors which, when added together, produce white light.
- Complementary colors are opposite of each other on the color wheel.
- Split complementary colors are three-color combinations with one color plus the two colors on either side of its complementary.
- Triads are three-color combinations that are equidistant apart on the color wheel.
- Analogous colors are side-by-side in the color wheel. They can be two-color combinations or three-color combinations.
- White can be combined with any color to create contrast of saturation, contrast of light and dark, or contrast of proportion.
- Single colors often evoke a strong emotion response based on color associations.

Words to Know

- Complementary – completing.
- Triad – a group of three.
- Analogous – similar or alike.
- Symbolism – representation by means of attributing meaning to an object.

Figure 34 - The contrast between the white light downstage on the artist and the colored light on the backdrop helps define the areas of the stage, giving it more dimension and depth. (Artist: Mark Schultz; Lighting design: Andrew Wakeman, Phil Gilbert, Richard Cadena; Production company: Maxx Productions)

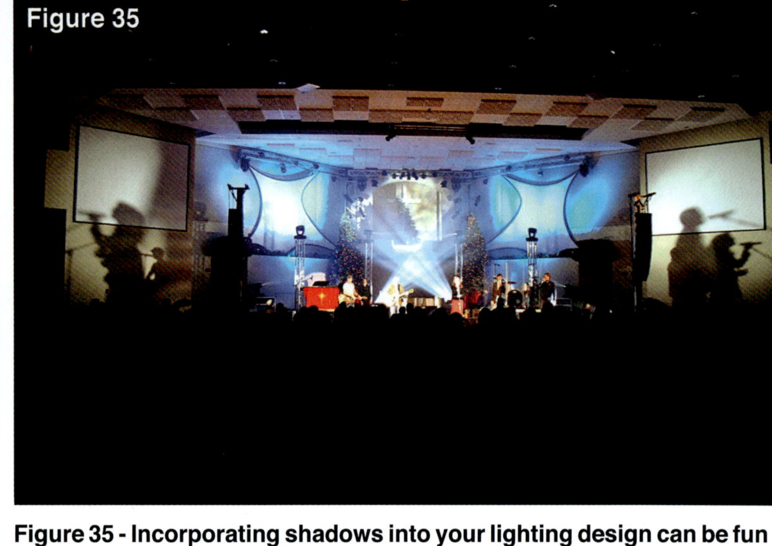

Figure 35 - Incorporating shadows into your lighting design can be fun and effective. (Artist: Watermark; Lighting design: Richard Cadena)

USING THE SEVEN CONTRASTS

By selecting the right lighting instruments and fitting them with a good selection of colors, diffusion and color correction, we can equip ourselves with the right tools to create the most effective lighting design possible. By using the seven contrasts pioneered by Itten, we can make the most of the lighting system.

With contrast of saturation we can emphasize the spatial relationship of all the parts of the stage – downstage, midstage and upstage. Lesser saturated colors appear to be farther away, as if viewing a distant horizon through a thin haze. More saturated colors appear to be closer. Alternatively, we can create depth by using white light downstage and colored light upstage.

The contrast of light and dark is a natural for the lighting designer, but by paying special attention to shadows you can elevate your art much as Leonardo da Vinci did by using chiaroscuro. Claude Debussy said, “Music is the silence between the notes.” By the same token, it’s the shadows that make great lighting come to the fore.

The contrast of proportion can help create new looks from old. By changing the proportion of one color in a multi-color look, we can totally change the feel of that look. In an environment where freshness and new ideas are highly valued, using proportion in our looks is like money in the bank. Many lighting designers go to great lengths to avoid repeating a look. Similarly, the Bezold Effect tells us that changing one color in a multiple-color composition changes the entire appearance.

The contrast of complements provides fertile ground for color combinations, hopefully not as a catalog of combinations from which to select like a Chinese menu, but a starting point

Figure 36 – Adding a color in a small proportion completely transforms the look of this sanctuary. (First Baptist Church, Sacramento; Lighting designer: Richard Cadena)

Figure 37 - The simultaneous contrast of the red/green is among the strongest of contrasts. (Artist: Shaun Groves; Lighting designer: Richard Cadena; Production company: Maxx Productions)

for sparking ideas and variations. Simultaneous contrast is a subset of complementary colors, except they are a special case whereby the combination is so vibrant as to create the illusion of motion and energy. The classic combination is red/green, although this combination is strongly associated with Christmas so it should be used appropriately.

Contrast of warm and cool is one of the keystones in the McCandless lighting method, which he used to help model the subject. Since the advent of color television, there has been some debate about the effectiveness of using warm and cool colors on opposing sides of the same subject. Some people believe that accurate color rendition models the face much better.

But the contrast of hues – the juxtaposition of two or more colors – is the lighting designer's stock in trade. It is the backbone of our compositions and the soul of our art. Learning how to use it effectively is tantamount to perfecting the craft of lighting design.

SUMMARY

After selecting lighting instruments and laying them out on a lighting plot, the selection of diffusion, color temperature and color is the most important aspect of lighting design. It's what gives the lighting rig its character and flexibility. The ability to control the quality of light – shadows, contrast, color, glare, etc. – is as important as the quantity, uniformity and direction of the lighting. These tasks are accomplished with the use of diffusion materials, gels and color selection. Although there is a lot of documentation and reading material available about these aspects of lighting design, experience is the best teacher. If we experiment with different uses and combinations of these tools we will come to know them well enough to apply them freely.

DOCUMENTATION AND PAPERWORK

"Where the spirit does not work with the hand there is no art."
— Leonardo da Vinci

Chapter 8

DOCUMENTATION AND PAPERWORK

The key to coordinating a successful lighting design project is good communication. And in the realm of construction, drawing is the universal language and paperwork is the de facto MapQuest. A complete set of construction drawings is what most architects, engineers, electrical contractors, and A/V contractors expect to see when they ask you to complete a lighting design project. How those documents are created and assembled can vary from designer to designer, but it helps if they bear a strong resemblance to the other architectural and construction drawings. And as long as you include certain ingredients – lighting plots, riser diagrams, equipment schedules, panel schedules, and perhaps some detail drawings – then they will.

The days have long passed when a draftsman used pencil and paper to create construction drawings. The overwhelming standard for architects and engineers is AutoCAD or a similar computer aided design software package. Most lighting designers today also use lighting design software that is very similar to AutoCAD but with specialized tools and features that help quicken the lighting design process. For example, all of the mechanical skills we learned in the first section, those bits about calculating illuminance, beam width, and throw distances can all be quickly deciphered by using lighting design software.

There are many such lighting design and documentation software packages on the market today. If you are totally unfamiliar with AutoCAD, then it's probably a good idea to start with something simple like SoftPlot (www.stageresearch.com) or WYSIWYG (www.cast-soft.com). On the other hand, if you have experience with AutoCAD or AutoCAD Lite then you might like the power and features of LD Assistant (www.ldassistant.com) or VectorWorks (www.nemetschek.net).

In addition to the drawing and plotting features, some of these software packages also have other features to help document our project including paperwork management, photo-realistic rendering capability, and visualization. Visualization is the ability to program a virtual scene or look without having to set up any lighting or control.

There are also stand-alone and plug-in software products like ESP Vision visualization software (www.espvision.com), Lightwright (www.mckernon.com), and Focus Track (www.focustrack.co.uk) paperwork management software. If you are unfamiliar with these products it would be a good idea to research them on the internet and try them out.

The following pages show some sample drawings and documents. You can use these as a guide to help you develop your own documentation or use them as a template to follow. Either way, you should strive to provide as much complete information as possible. In the construction world, there's no such thing as too much information.

LIGHTING PLOTS

The lighting plot is the starting point for all of our drawings and documentation. It should clearly show a scaled representation of the sanctuary and the entire lighting system with the location of each light represented as a two-dimensional symbol. If we are using a lighting design software package then it will probably come with a library of symbols for commonly used fixtures. If the fixtures we need are not in the library, we can download a 2D or 3D symbol from the manufacturer's web site. The symbols should be simple and small in file size; large symbols can significantly slow down our computer if we're working on a large lighting system with lots of fixtures.

Figure 38

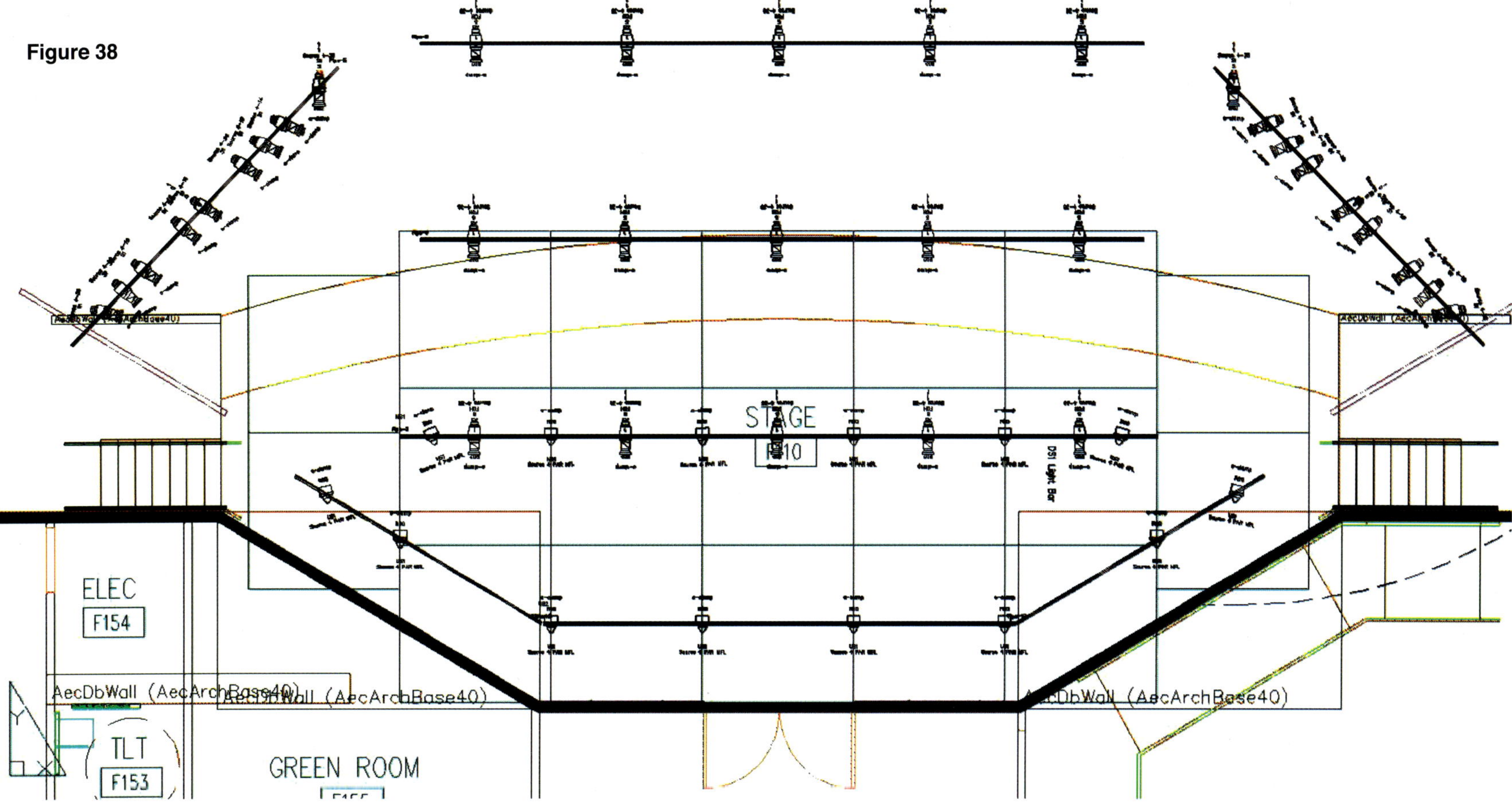

Figure 38 - Typical lighting plot showing fixture locations.

We generally start our lighting plot with a floor plan of the building. If we're working with new construction then the architect can usually supply an AutoCAD drawing of the building in a *.DWG or *.DXF file format as a starting point for our design. If we're using a software program other than AutoCAD then we might have to use the import feature to bring it into the drawing. Is some cases, a DWG or DXF file may not import 100% correctly, so we should be sure to check it carefully after importing. We can get an idea of how well it imports by checking the dimensions of the drawing after it is imported.

If we're working with an existing building then we may or may not be able to get copies of the plans, and even if we do, they might exist only in blueprint form and not in electronic format. In that case we might have to re-create the drawing in AutoCAD or in our lighting design software. However, if there are no drawings at all – and that does happen – we will have to take measurements in the building and draw it from scratch. In the event that we have to undertake this step, a laser distance meter will speed up the process tremendously.

2D AND 3D DRAWINGS

Once we have a two-dimensional plan view of the space in which we will be designing a lighting system, then we should consider using it to create a three-dimensional model with the walls, platform, soft goods (curtains, borders, legs, etc.), seating, video screens, and anything else that might be important to the project. We will need this information after the layout is complete and we start focusing, checking sight lines, and eventually applying materials to create photo-realistic renderings.

With our lighting design software, we should be able to extrude walls, stairs, columns, the platform, risers, and any other construction elements. We can also create curtains, borders, legs, and other masking soft goods. Lastly, we can add seating before we start layout out the lighting and rigging.

ATTRIBUTE DATABASE

In addition to showing the locations of each fixture, the lighting plot should also have a database containing a number attributes associated with each fixture. Some of the more common attributes associated with conventional lighting that should be in the database include: position, unit number, type, channel, dimmer, circuit, color, focus, iris/gobo, accessory, purpose, candle power, field angle, beam angle, wattage, price, lamp, weight, and possibly more. Each of these attributes is explained in more detail below:

Position – Each location in the plot should carry an identifier and each fixture should be labeled according its position. For example, if a fixture is 10 feet off the center line, stage right on the upstage truss, then we might label the position US-10SR or a similar designation.

Unit – Each fixture should have a unique unit number starting with 1. It's a good idea to get into the habit of using a standard convention, even if it's our own, to label the unit numbers. For example, we can start with the fixture that is farthest downstage right and work our way through upstage left.

Type – This is the fixture type, e.g., Altman Shakespeare 30 degree.

Channel – The console will eventually need to be patched to map each control channel to a fixture. The channel number is a patching map that we create during the design process. It is useful to get into the habit of grouping like fixtures to certain channels, e.g., conventional fixtures start at channel 1 and automated fixtures start at channel 200, etc.

Dimmer – Conventional fixtures have to be controlled through a dimmer and this attribute assigns the fixture to a dimmer. This is different than the channel number in that the channel is on the console while the dimmer is on the dimmer rack. Sometimes the channel and dimmer numbers are identical and sometimes they aren't.

Circuit – The circuit number helps the electrician terminate the dimming circuit from the dimmer to the fixture. If each wire is labeled according to your plot, then everyone from the electrician to the A/V installer will have an easier time ringing out the system and commissioning it.

Color – The color is a gel number indicating which gels are to be fitted in each fixture.

Focus – The focus is a reference indicating where on the platform the fixture should be focused. It comes in very handy after we focus the plot and come back to it at a later time. It helps us to remember where each light should be focused. We shouldn't neglect to use this feature or we will eventually regret it.

Iris/gobo – In case we add an iris or gobo pattern, this attribute indicates in which fixtures they go.

Accessory – Any other accessories, such as a color scroller or gobo rotator, can be indicated here.

Purpose – This attribute helps us identify all of your key lights, fill lights, backlights, cyc lights, architectural lights, footlights, etc.

Candle Power – If our software has this attribute it can be a huge time saver. Some lighting design packages calculate the illuminance automatically after we focus the cone of light or line emanating from the fixture. The candle power is often available on the manufacturer's web site and we should always verify the data before finalizing a plot.

Field Angle and Beam Angle – In addition to calculating the illuminance, most lighting design software will also give us a visual representation of the beam and field after we focus a fixture. It might also give us a numerical readout as well.

Wattage – The fixture wattage is necessary in order for the electrical engineer to perform their load calculations. This feature helps us keep track of the system loads. We can get this data from spec sheets on the manufacturer's web site.

Price – Keeping track of the budget is almost always a necessity when we're working on a lighting design for a church. This attribute helps you assemble the final budget number by tracking each light individually.

Lamp – In addition to helping keep track of which lamps we specify, this attribute also helps the installer to make sure they put the right lamps (long life of course!) in the right fixtures.

Weight – It is extremely important to keep track of the amount of weight you're putting on each truss or pipe. This attribute helps us track individual weights in order to turn over the data to a rigger or structural engineer. We really don't want to be responsible for an accident due to a structural failure.

All of these attributes are stored for each fixture, and custom schedules can be exported and massaged in order to manage different aspects of our design. For example, we might want to export a fixture list with the associated prices in order to calculate the cost of the entire system. Other examples include schedules for patching the console, terminating the wiring, focusing fixtures, cutting gels, calculating the system electrical load, or creating a list for the purchasing agent.

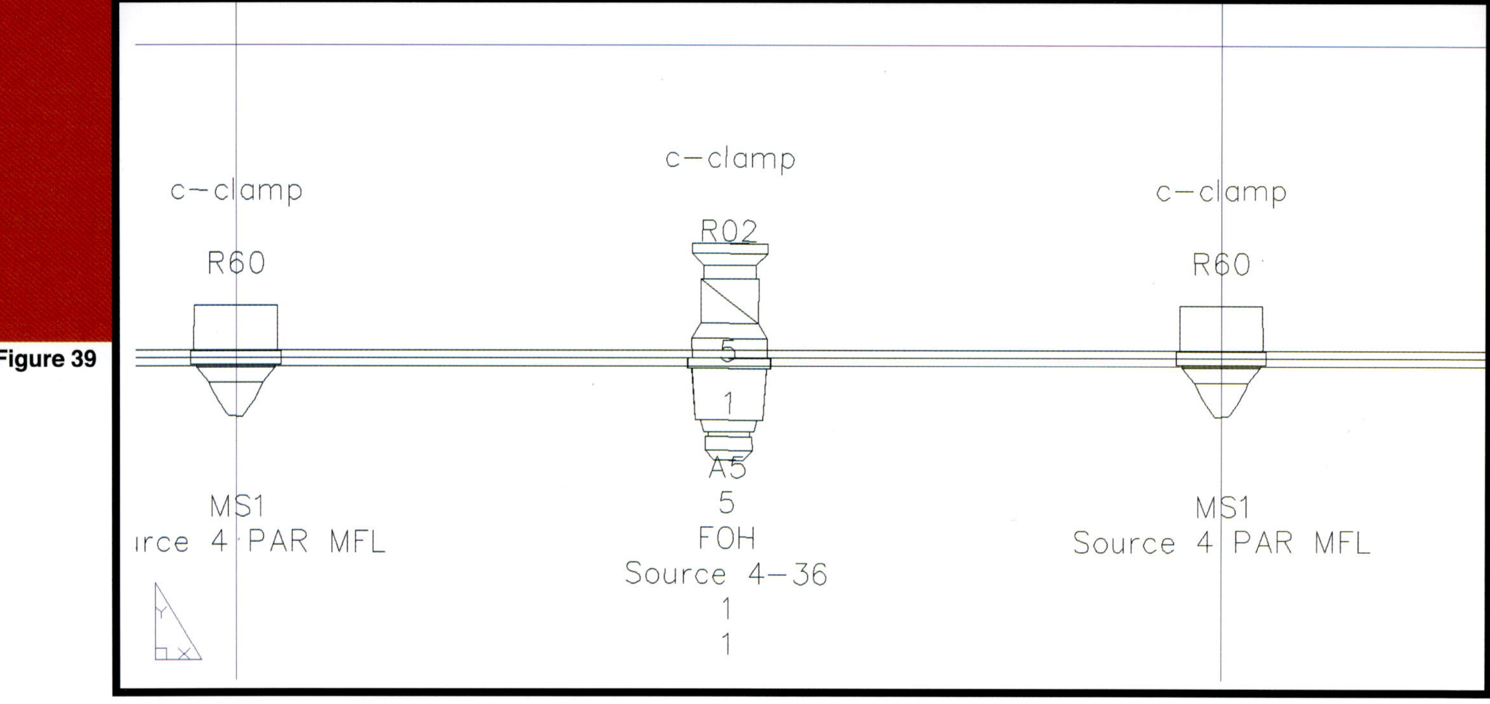

Figure 39 - Individual attributes for each fixture type can be visible or hidden depending on the purpose of the plot.

The software can be configured so that each attribute is either visible or hidden on the lighting plot. Whether or not an attribute is shown depends on the purpose of the plot: e.g., a focus plot need not indicate fixture costs. Even if the attribute is not visible on the plot, it is still in the database.

Once we have finished building our 3D model and the lighting and rigging is all in place, then we will want to plot the design on paper. In North America, construction drawings are typically plotted on architectural-sized paper. The more common sizes are 36" x 48" "Arch E" size paper and 24" x 36" "Arch D" size paper. They should be plotted in architectural units (inches and fractions of an inch) to scale and the scale should be indicated in the title block.

A complete set of drawings usually includes three different perspectives of the lighting plot: a plan view (looking down on the drawing as if the roof were removed and we're hovering above the building), an elevation (looking at a section of the building as if we're standing on the floor, except it shows no depth perception), and an isometric view (from an angle so we can see the top and the sides simultaneously). If our software allows us to create multiple view ports on one sheet, we might want to put all three perspectives on a single page provided the detail is not obscured or too small to read.

Concepts:

- Computer aided design (CAD) software is the industry standard for creating construction drawings.
- Photo-realistic rendering is a computer representation of a real world object or objects. Many lighting design software packages allow you to create a lighting system in a 3D model and render it to the monitor or printer.
- Visualization is a computer representation of a lighting system that allows you to program looks and scenes in virtual reality. Many lighting design software packages provide the ability to program entire shows with visualization.
- An attribute database typically contains all of the relevant data for each light in a lighting system. It is used to create various schedules for a number of different purposes.
- A lighting plot is a scaled drawing of a lighting system showing the exact locations of each lighting instrument.

Words to Know

- AutoCAD – computer aided design software made by AutoDesk.
- Soft goods – curtains, borders, legs, and backdrops made of cloth.
- Attribute database – a database with a list of lighting instruments and their attributes such as luminous intensity, beam angle, field angle, weight, etc.
- View port – a window in a drawing.
- Arch E sized paper – 36" x 48" plotting paper.
- Arch D sized paper – 24" x 36" plotting paper.

RENDERINGS

A rendering is a computer simulation that is used to illustrate how the finished design might look. Sometimes, but not always, a rendering or set of renderings is included in the documentation. It may be necessary to create these renderings if they are needed to pitch a design or sell our services for a particular design. Other times the church just wants an idea of what to expect, especially if they are concerned about the how the lighting will blend with the architecture.

Renderings are usually created from AutoCAD drawings or directly in lighting design software. The most photo-realistic renderings are created using several different programs such as AutoCAD (or lighting design CAD), Photoshop, and 3D Studio Max. They start with a 3D model and then "materials" are "applied" to the surface of each object. The materials are nothing more than bitmaps or JPEGs of real world materials such as wood, carpet, metal, etc. The materials to be applied might be pulled from a library provided by the software manufacturer or third-party supplier. Alternatively, we can take pictures of real materials, preferably from the actual room if it is existing construction, and use them to apply to the surfaces of our 3D model. For example, in the illustration to the right, stained glass windows and pipe organ tubes would have been very difficult to draw in AutoCAD. Instead, pictures were taken of the windows and pipes, and they were cropped to create a small bitmap for each item. The bitmaps were then applied to flat surfaces to make the model look more true to life. Once all the materials are applied, the computer renders the image.

Figure 40

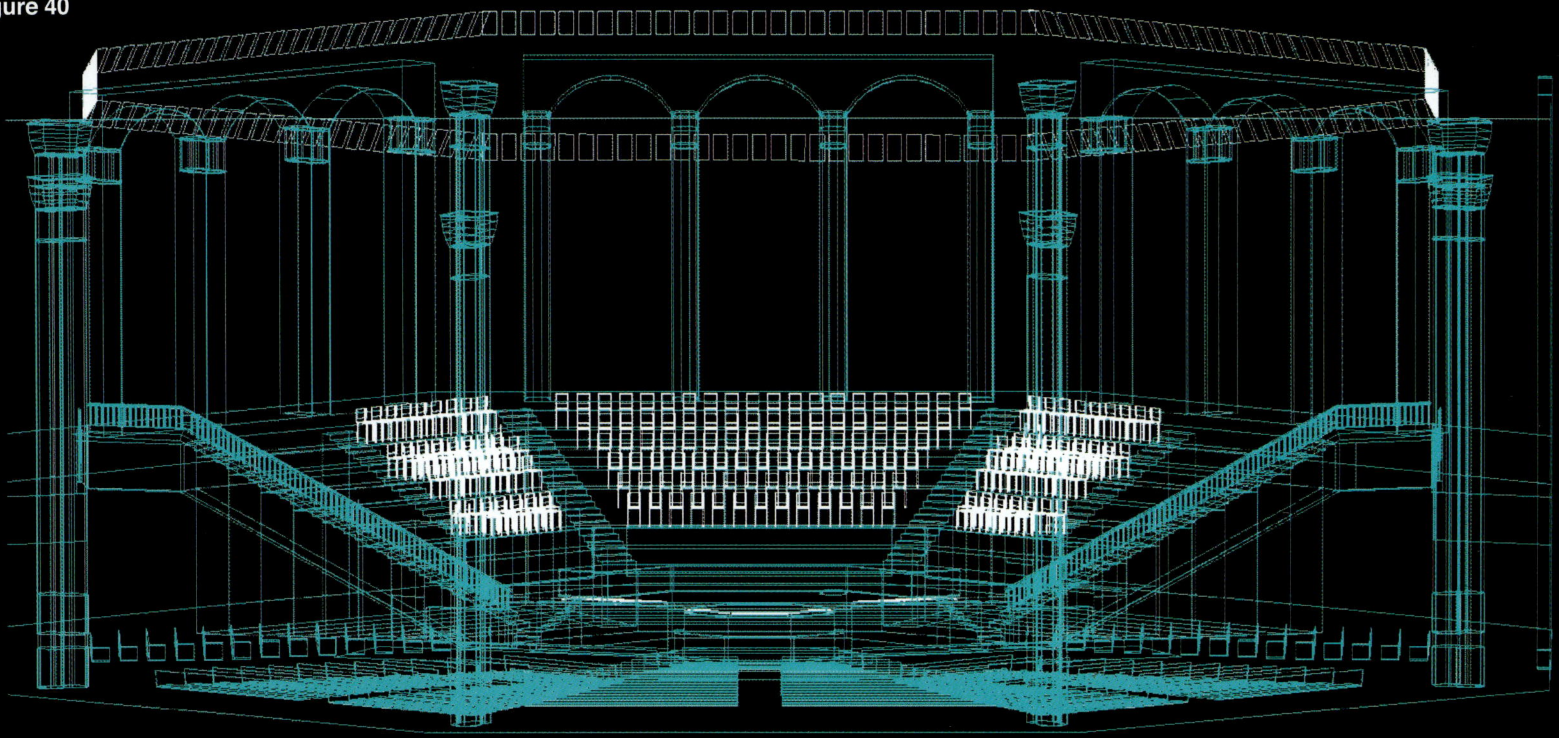

Figure 40 – Wire frame 3D model of Second Baptist Church in Houston, Texas.

Figure 41

Figure 41 - The same computer model as shown above, except this model is rendered with materials applied to the surface of each object. The stained glass windows and pipe organs are actual photos applied to the model.

Figure 42

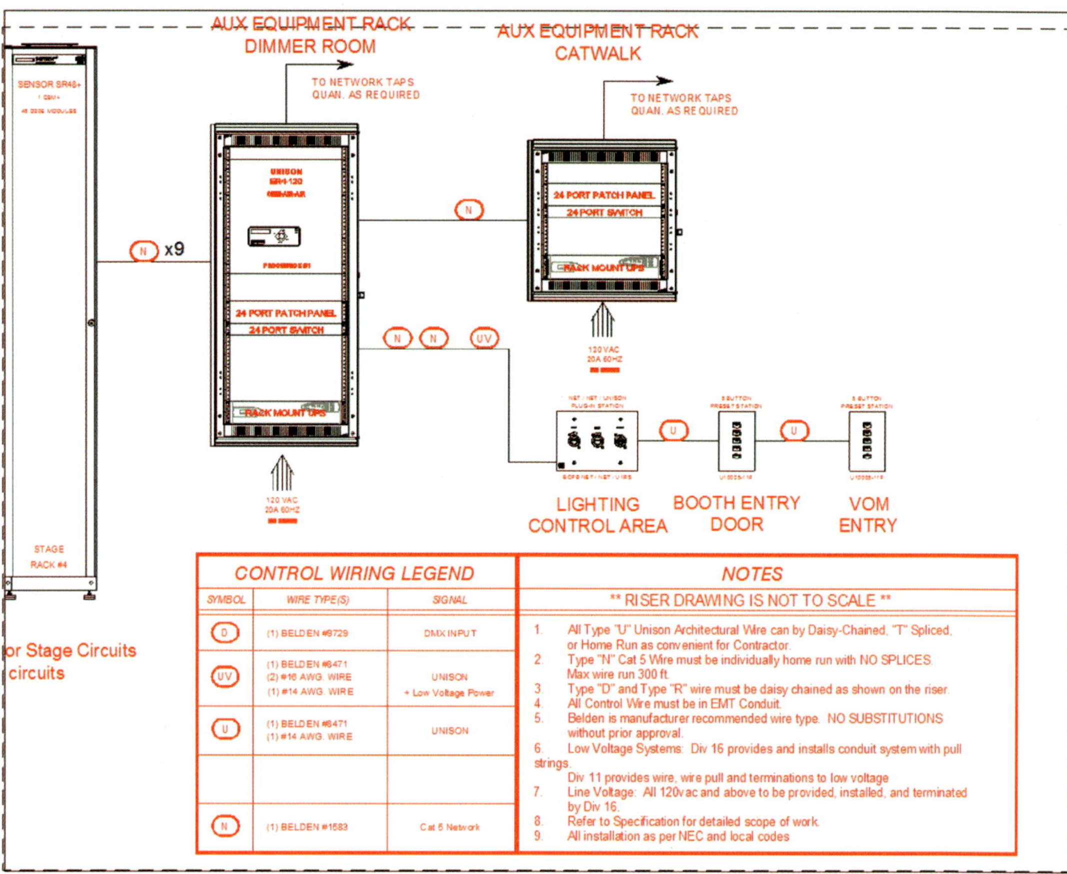

Figure 42 - Riser diagram showing low voltage network schematic diagram and wiring legend. (Courtesy of ETC and Edwin Jones Co., Inc.)

RISER DIAGRAMS

A riser diagram is a schematic representation of the wiring in a system from the feeder cable up to but not including individual branch circuits. Riser diagrams are commonly used to illustrate the system integration of lighting, control systems, networks, or any associated wired or wireless system. They are very important in the documentation of a complete lighting system because they provide a reference for the construction crew to understand how the system is supposed to interconnect.

A riser diagram is not drawn to scale; rather, it is typically shown as a single line connecting elements of a system. In a lighting system, there are typically two independent but related systems that show up in a riser diagram; the high voltage system and the low voltage system. By "high voltage," we mean greater than 50 volts. This includes the electrical power distribution, dimming, and luminaires. The low voltage system typically includes the controller(s), data distribution network, Ethernet network, and wall control panels.

Riser diagrams vary in style so it's a good idea to study the works of others to get a good idea of how it's done. The easiest to read and understand typically show accurate drawings of the larger components like breaker panels, dimmer racks, and equipment cabinets and a single-line connecting them. The cabling should be clearly labeled and the legend should call out specific cable and wire types with notes to help the technicians and electricians install the system correctly.

EQUIPMENT SCHEDULES

One of the most useful features of an attribute database is that it gives us the ability to export a variety of schedules for various purposes. The attribute for each light can be used or not used, depending on the purpose of a particular schedule. For example, if we want a simple equipment schedule to calculate costs for budgeting reasons, then we can list only the fixture type and its associated cost. We can also total the fixture count and create a condensed equipment list with the total cost of lighting package.

As we progress in our lighting design, a few different schedules are likely to be useful to us. In the design phase, we will more than likely need a schedule of equipment and accessories with their associated cost to evaluate the budget. Once the budget is finalized and the equipment list approved, then we might need to supply the electrical contractor with our electrical load requirements. They, in turn, might give the electrical load schedule to an electrical engineer to evaluate the ability of the power distribution equipment to handle the load and to generate an electrical one-line diagram, showing all of the electrical distribution equipment, in order to pull a permit from the city or the proper code enforcement jurisdiction.

Figure 43

Sample Equipment Schedule

Position	Unit	Type	Channel	Dimmer	Circuit	Color	Focus	Purpose	Wattage	Price	Lamp	Weight	Misc 1	Hardware	Power
DS1	24	Source 4-36	24	24	24	R02	MS1	key light	575	385	HPL 575/115X	14	L5-15 male connector	safety cable	575
DS1	25	Source 4-36	25	25	25	R02	MS2	key light	575	385	HPL 575/115X	14	L5-15 male connector	safety cable	575
DS1	26	Source 4-36	26	26	26	R02	MS3	key light	575	385	HPL 575/115X	14	L5-15 male connector	safety cable	575
DS1	27	Source 4-36	27	27	27	R02	MS4	key light	575	385	HPL 575/115X	14	L5-15 male connector	safety cable	575
DS1	28	Source 4-36	28	28	28	R02	MS5	key light	575	385	HPL 575/115X	14	L5-15 male connector	safety cable	575
DS1	105	Robe ColorWash 575AT			ND3	-	-	automated wash	800	5073	MSD 575	71	L5-15 male connector	safety cable	800
DS1	106	Robe ColorWash 575AT			ND3	-	-	automated wash	800	5073	MSD 575	71	L5-15 male connector	safety cable	800
DS1	107	Robe ColorWash 575AT			ND4	-	-	automated wash	800	5073	MSD 575	71	L5-15 male connector	safety cable	800
DS1	108	Robe ColorWash 575AT			ND4	-	-	automated wash	800	5073	MSD 575	71	L5-15 male connector	safety cable	800
FOH	10	Source 4-36	10	10	10	R02	DS2	key light	575	385	HPL 575/115X	14	L5-15 male connector	safety cable	575
FOH	11	Source 4-36	11	11	11	R02	DS3	key light	575	385	HPL 575/115X	14	L5-15 male connector	safety cable	575
FOH	12	Source 4-36	12	12	12	R02	DS4	key light	575	385	HPL 575/115X	14	L5-15 male connector	safety cable	575
FOH	13	Source 4-36	13	13	13	R02	DS5	key light	575	385	HPL 575/115X	14	L5-15 male connector	safety cable	575
FOH	14	Source 4-36	14	14	14	R02	DS6	key light	575	385	HPL 575/115X	14	L5-15 male connector	safety cable	575
FOH	101	Robe ColorSpot 575AT			ND1	-	-	automated spot	800	5073	MSD 575	80	L5-15 male connector	safety cable	800
FOH	102	Robe ColorSpot 575AT			ND1	-	-	automated spot	800	5073	MSD 575	80	L5-15 male connector	safety cable	800
FOH	103	Robe ColorSpot 575AT			ND2	-	-	automated spot	800	5073	MSD 575	80	L5-15 male connector	safety cable	800
FOH	104	Robe ColorSpot 575AT			ND2	-	-	automated spot	800	5073	MSD 575	80	L5-15 male connector	safety cable	800
MS1	29	Source 4 PAR MFL	29	29	29	R60	DS1/2	backlight	575	194	HPL 575/115X	7.5	L5-15 male connector	safety cable	575
MS1	30	Source 4-36	30	30	30	R02	US2	key light	575	385	HPL 575/115X	14	L5-15 male connector	safety cable	575
MS1	31	Source 4 PAR MFL	31	31	31	R60	DS2/3	backlight	575	194	HPL 575/115X	7.5	L5-15 male connector	safety cable	575
MS1	32	Source 4-36	32	32	32	R02	US3	key light	575	385	HPL 575/115X	14	L5-15 male connector	safety cable	575
MS1	33	Source 4 PAR MFL	33	33	33	R60	DS3/4	backlight	575	194	HPL 575/115X	7.5	L5-15 male connector	safety cable	575
MS1	34	Source 4-36	34	34	34	R02	US4	key light	575	385	HPL 575/115X	14	L5-15 male connector	safety cable	575
MS1	35	Source 4 PAR MFL	35	35	35	R60	DS4/5	backlight	575	194	HPL 575/115X	7.5	L5-15 male connector	safety cable	575
MS1	36	Source 4-36	36	36	36	R02	US5	key light	575	385	HPL 575/115X	14	L5-15 male connector	safety cable	575
MS1	37	Source 4 PAR MFL	37	37	37	R60	DS5/6	backlight	575	194	HPL 575/115X	7.5	L5-15 male connector	safety cable	575
MS1	38	Source 4-36	38	38	38	R02	US6	key light	575	385	HPL 575/115X	14	L5-15 male connector	safety cable	575
MS1	39	Source 4 PAR MFL	39	39	39	R60	DS6/7	backlight	575	194	HPL 575/115X	7.5	L5-15 male connector	safety cable	575
S1	1	Source 4-36	1	1	1	R51	DS1	fill light	575	385	HPL 575/115X	14	L5-15 male connector	safety cable	575
S1	2	Source 4-19	2	2	2	R51	US2	fill light	575	385	HPL 575/115X	14	L5-15 male connector	safety cable	575
S1	3	Source 4-19	3	3	3	R51	US3/4	fill light	575	385	HPL 575/115X	14	L5-15 male connector	safety cable	575
S1	4	Source 4-19	4	4	4	R51	MS1	fill light	575	385	HPL 575/115X	14	L5-15 male connector	safety cable	575
S1	5	Source 4-19	5	5	5	R51	MS2/US	fill light	575	385	HPL 575/115X	14	L5-15 male connector	safety cable	575
S1	6	Source 4-26	6	6	6	R51	DS2	fill light	575	385	HPL 575/115X	14	L5-15 male connector	safety cable	575
S1	7	Source 4-19	7	7	7	R51	DS3	fill light	575	385	HPL 575/115X	14	L5-15 male connector	safety cable	575
S1	8	Source 4-14	8	8	8	R51	DS4/5	fill light	575	385	HPL 575/115X	14	L5-15 male connector	safety cable	575
S1	9	Source 4-36	9	9	9	R02	DS1	key light	575	385	HPL 575/115X	14	L5-15 male connector	safety cable	575
S2	15	Source 4-36	15	15	15	R02	DS7	key light	575	385	HPL 575/115X	14	L5-15 male connector	safety cable	575
S2	16	Source 4-14	16	16	16	R51	DS4/3	fill light	575	385	HPL 575/115X	14	L5-15 male connector	safety cable	575
S2	17	Source 4-19	17	17	17	R51	DS5	fill light	575	385	HPL 575/115X	14	L5-15 male connector	safety cable	575
S2	18	Source 4-26	18	18	18	R51	DS6	fill light	575	385	HPL 575/115X	14	L5-15 male connector	safety cable	575
S2	19	Source 4-19	19	19	19	R51	MS5/US	fill light	575	385	HPL 575/115X	14	L5-15 male connector	safety cable	575
S2	20	Source 4-19	20	20	20	R51	MS5	fill light	575	385	HPL 575/115X	14	L5-15 male connector	safety cable	575
S2	21	Source 4-19	21	21	21	R51	US5/4	fill light	575	385	HPL 575/115X	14	L5-15 male connector	safety cable	575
S2	22	Source 4-19	22	22	22	R51	US6	fill light	575	385	HPL 575/115X	14	L5-15 male connector	safety cable	575
S2	23	Source 4-36	23	23	23	R51	DS7	fill light	575	385	HPL 575/115X	14	L5-15 male connector	safety cable	575
US1	40	Source 4 PAR MFL	40	40	40	R60	DS1	backlight	575	194	HPL 575/115X	7.5	L5-15 male connector	safety cable	575
US1	41	Source 4 PAR MFL	41	41	41	R60	US1/MS	backlight	575	194	HPL 575/115X	7.5	L5-15 male connector	safety cable	575
US1	42	Source 4 PAR MFL	42	42	42	R60	MS1/2	backlight	575	194	HPL 575/115X	7.5	L5-15 male connector	safety cable	575
US1	43	Source 4 PAR MFL	43	43	43	R60	MS2/3	backlight	575	194	HPL 575/115X	7.5	L5-15 male connector	safety cable	575
US1	44	Source 4 PAR MFL	44	44	44	R60	MS3/4	backlight	575	194	HPL 575/115X	7.5	L5-15 male connector	safety cable	575
US1	45	Source 4 PAR MFL	45	45	45	R60	MS4/5	backlight	575	194	HPL 575/115X	7.5	L5-15 male connector	safety cable	575
US1	46	Source 4 PAR MFL	46	46	46	R60	MS5/US	backlight	575	194	HPL 575/115X	7.5	L5-15 male connector	safety cable	575
US1	47	Source 4 PAR MFL	47	47	47	R60	DS7	backlight	575	194	HPL 575/115X	7.5	L5-15 male connector	safety cable	575
									43025	116881		2095	67	55	33425

Figure 43 - Sample equipment schedule showing total wattage, total cost, total weight, and more.

Next, we might generate another equipment schedule showing the weights of each individual fixture and the total weight of each pipe or truss to provide to the structural engineer for their calculations. We might also want to generate a schedule showing the gel requirements including colors, sizes, the associated luminaire, and its location. A little manipulation of the schedule generator and we should be able to print and e-mail a custom schedule tailored to the need at hand.

Lighting Breaker Panel A

Description: Non-dim lighting circuits											
Bus Amps: 160 amps three-phase											
Volts/ Phase: 120/ 208V, 3-phase, 4-wire plus ground											
Service: Auditorium F111											
Location: ELEC F154											
Ckt. No.	**Description**	**Lamp Type**	**Load (VA)**	**Breaker Amps**	**Breaker Pole**	**Wire No.**	**Phase**	**Wire No.**	**Breaker Pole**	**Breaker Amps**	**Load (V**
ND-1	2 x Robe ColorSpot 575AT	discharge	1520	20	1	1	A	2	1	20	152
ND-3	2 x Robe ColorWash 575AT	discharge	1520	20	1	3	B	4	1	20	152
ND-5	2 x Robe ColorSpot 575AT	discharge	1520	20	1	5	C	6	1	20	152
ND-7	2 x Robe ColorWash 575AT	discharge	1520	20	1	7	A	8	1	20	152
ND-9	2 x Robe ColorSpot 575AT	discharge	1520	20	1	9	B	10	1	20	152
-	SPARE	-	-			-	C	-			-
-	SPARE	-	-			-	A	-			-
-	SPARE	-	-			-	B	-			-
-	SPARE	-	-			-	C	-			-
-	SPARE	-	-			-	A	-			-
-	SPARE	-	-			-	B	-			-
-	SPARE	-	-			-	C	-			-
Total Connected Load: 15,200VA											

Figure 44 - Breaker panel schedule showing terminations for each circuit. A description of each of these bits of information follows:

Once construction starts, then we can provide custom schedules to the electricians showing each fixture, its wire number, and the general location of the dimmer circuits. We might provide the A/V installers with an equipment list showing the gel colors and diffusion to be cut and loaded in each instrument and which hardware and accessories are required for each. As they hang the plot, we can provide yet another schedule showing the position and the focus of each light so they can rough it in. And finally, we can generate a patch schedule to provide the programmer in order to patch the console and set the dimmer addresses.

PANEL SCHEDULES

In addition to equipment schedules, it is a good idea to provide panel schedules to guide the electricians through the project. A panel schedule standard to every electrical installation. What's unique about our panel schedules is that, in addition to breaker panel schedules, we also have dimmer panel schedules with which to be concerned.

Most commercial electricians have little experience with theatrical lighting, dimming, and control and they typically have many questions about the equipment that is going to be connected to the system they are installing. By providing them with this extra bit of information you can help them understand the scope of the project and how it is supposed to work.

BREAKER PANEL SCHEDULES

A breaker panel schedule serves two basic purposes: it illustrates which circuits are to be connected to which breakers, and it shows the type of load to be connected. For example, it indicates whether a load is a purely resistive load like an incandescent lamp or an inductive load like a motor or a transformer. This information helps an engineer or electrician

Figure 44

...mp Type	Description	Ckt. No.
...scharge	2 x Robe ColorSpot 575AT	ND-2
...scharge	2 x Robe ColorWash 575AT	ND-4
...scharge	2 x Robe ColorSpot 575AT	ND-6
...scharge	2 x Robe ColorWash 575AT	ND-8
...scharge	2 x Robe ColorSpot 575AT	ND-10
	SPARE	-
	SPARE	-
	SPARE	-
	SPARE	-
	SPARE	-
	SPARE	-
	SPARE	-

evaluate the total connected load and whether the supply is sufficient to safely provide the power requirements.

A breaker panel schedule should have the following information: panel label, description, bus amps (the size of the bus bar supplying the current), voltage and phase arrangement, service location, and location label (on architectural drawings). In addition, it should also give a description of each load to be connected to each circuit and the associated circuit number, the load type, the V-A rating, the breaker size, the wire number, and the phase to which each load is connected.

- Panel label: Name of the breaker panel. If there is not already an assigned name, choose something that is logical.
- Description: Describe the purpose of the breaker panel. In our case, it is almost always for non-dim theatrical lighting circuits.
- Bus amps: Every panel board has a bus bar (a copper bar used to distribute electricity) with a rated value in amps. This is the bus amps.
- Voltage and phase: The voltage and type of service, e.g. single-phase, two-phase, or three-phase. This description should also include the number of wires, e.g., 3-wire (hot, neutral, and ground), 4-wire (two hots, neutral, and ground), or 5-wire (three hots, neutral, and ground).
- Service and location: The area in which electrical service is to be supplied and its associated label as indicated on the blueprints.
- Circuit number: The circuit number as assigned on the lighting plot. This is different than the wire number.
- Description: This is a description of the connected load, e.g. incandescent lights or chain motors.
- Load type: The engineer needs to know whether the connected load is a resistive load like an incandescent lamp, a capacitive load like anything with a switch-mode power supply, or an inductive load like a motor or a transformer. This information helps the engineer evaluate the load in terms of the power factor (the phase angle between the voltage and current) and the harmonics that could feed back through the neutral. That, in turn, helps the engineer design the system properly.
- Load (VA): The "apparent" power is the voltage times the current in amps. This is close to the wattage of the load except it takes into account the phase angle between the voltage and current. This information is often supplied in the specs of the device to be connected.
- Breaker amps: This is the rated value of the breaker to which the load is connected.
- Breaker pole: In North America, a single pole breaker is used with a 120V load and a two-pole breaker is used with a 208V load.
- Wire number: This is the number we assigned during the design process to help the electrician keep track of all the circuits.
- Phase: In a three-phase panel, there are three hot feeds labeled "A," "B," and "C." Each of these hot legs is 120 degrees out of phase with each other, thus the nomenclature.

Note that the even numbered circuits in the panel schedule mirror the odd numbered circuits. That is because two breakers share the same phase and they are physically laid out across from each other. The graphic layout of the panel schedule reflects the physical layout.

Figure 45

Dimmer Rack Termination Schedule								
Description: 4 x Leprecon MX-1200 12-channel dimmer pack, 1.2KW/ channel								
Bus Amps: 4 x 40 amps three phase								
Volts/ Phase: 120/ 208V, 3-phase, 4-wire plus ground								
Service: Auditorium F111								
Location: ELEC F154								
Ckt. No.	Description	Lamp Type	VA/ Phase			Wire No.	Bkr. Amp	Comments
			A	B	C			
A1	ETC Source Four Leko 36°	Incandescent	575			1	20	
A2	ETC Source Four Leko 19°	Incandescent		575		2	20	
A3	ETC Source Four Leko 19°	Incandescent			575	3	20	
A4	ETC Source Four Leko 19°	Incandescent	575			4	20	
A5	ETC Source Four Leko 19°	Incandescent		575		5	20	
A6	ETC Source Four Leko 26°	Incandescent			575	6	20	
A7	ETC Source Four Leko 19°	Incandescent	575			7	20	
A8	ETC Source Four Leko 14°	Incandescent		575		8	20	
A9	ETC Source Four Leko 36°	Incandescent			575	9	20	
A10	ETC Source Four Leko 36°	Incandescent	575			10	20	
A11	ETC Source Four Leko 36°	Incandescent		575		11	20	
A12	ETC Source Four Leko 36°	Incandescent			575	12	20	
B1	ETC Source Four Leko 36°	Incandescent	575			13	20	
B2	ETC Source Four Leko 36°	Incandescent		575		14	20	
B3	ETC Source Four Leko 36°	Incandescent			575	15	20	
B4	ETC Source Four Leko 14°	Incandescent	575			16	20	
B5	ETC Source Four Leko 19°	Incandescent		575		17	20	
B6	ETC Source Four Leko 26°	Incandescent			575	18	20	
B7	ETC Source Four Leko 19°	Incandescent	575			19	20	
B8	ETC Source Four Leko 19°	Incandescent		575		20	20	
B9	ETC Source Four Leko 19°	Incandescent			575	21	20	
B10	ETC Source Four Leko 19°	Incandescent	575			22	20	
B11	ETC Source Four Leko 36°	Incandescent		575		23	20	
B12	ETC Source Four Leko 36°	Incandescent			575	24	20	
C1	ETC Source Four Leko 36°	Incandescent	575			25	20	
C2	ETC Source Four Leko 36°	Incandescent		575		26	20	
C3	ETC Source Four Leko 36°	Incandescent			575	27	20	
C4	ETC Source Four Leko 36°	Incandescent	575			28	20	
C5	ETC Source Four PAR MFL	Incandescent		575		29	20	
C6	ETC Source Four Leko 36°	Incandescent			575	30	20	
C7	ETC Source Four PAR MFL	Incandescent	575			31	20	
C8	ETC Source Four Leko 36°	Incandescent		575		32	20	
C9	ETC Source Four PAR MFL	Incandescent			575	33	20	
C10	ETC Source Four Leko 36°	Incandescent	575			34	20	
C11	ETC Source Four PAR MFL	Incandescent		575		35	20	
C12	ETC Source Four Leko 36°	Incandescent			575	36	20	
D1	ETC Source Four PAR MFL	Incandescent	575			37	20	
D2	ETC Source Four Leko 36°	Incandescent		575		38	20	
D3	ETC Source Four PAR MFL	Incandescent			575	39	20	
D4	ETC Source Four PAR MFL	Incandescent	575			40	20	
D5	ETC Source Four PAR MFL	Incandescent		575		41	20	
D6	ETC Source Four PAR MFL	Incandescent			575	42	20	
D7	ETC Source Four PAR MFL	Incandescent	575			43	20	
D8	ETC Source Four PAR MFL	Incandescent		575		44	20	
D9	ETC Source Four PAR MFL	Incandescent			575	45	20	
D10	ETC Source Four PAR MFL	Incandescent	575			46	20	
D11	ETC Source Four PAR MFL	Incandescent		575		47	20	
D12	SPARE	Incandescent			-	-	-	
Total Connected Load: 27,026VA								

Figure 45 - Sample dimmer panel schedule.

DIMMER PANEL SCHEDULES

The dimmer schedule is similar to the breaker panel schedule except that the phases are laid out sequentially rather than by even and odd circuit numbers. An example dimmer panel schedule is shown below.

It's easier to use an Excel spreadsheet to create a panel schedule than it is to use a CAD program because we can take advantage of features like autofill, cut and paste, etc.

Figure 46

Device Schedule							
Device	Type	ID	Quan	Circuit Type	Quan	Outlet Type	Notes
CSA1	18' Conector Strip						Left Feed
		DRA 1-14	14	20A Dimmed	14	24" Stage Pin Pigtail	
		TLI 1	1	120v Constant Power	2	L5-20 Flush	
			1	ETC NET	1	RJ45	
CSA2	18' Conector Strip						Right Feed
		DRA 15-28	14	20A Dimmed	14	24" Stage Pin Pigtail	
		TLI 2	1	120v Constant Power	2	L5-20 Flush	
			1	ETC NET	1	RJ45	
CSB1	18' Conector Strip						Left Feed
		DRA 29-38	10	20A Dimmed	10	24" Stage Pin Pigtail	
		TLI 3	1	120v Constant Power	2	L5-20 Flush	
			1	ETC NET	1	RJ45	
		WL1 361	1	20A Switched	2	L5-20 Flush	
CSB2	18' Conector Strip						Right Feed
		DRA 39-64	26	20A Dimmed	26	24" Stage Pin Pigtail	
		TLI 4	1	120v Constant Power	2	L5-20 Flush	
			1	ETC NET	1	RJ45	
CSC1	18' Conector Strip						Left Feed
		DRA 65-70	6	20A Dimmed	6	24" Stage Pin Pigtail	
		TLI 5	1	120v Constant Power	2	L5-20 Flush	
			1	ETC NET	1	RJ45	
		WL2 362	1	20A Switched	2	L5-20 Flush	
CSC2	18' Conector Strip						Right Feed
		DRA 71-80	10	20A Dimmed	10	24" Stage Pin Pigtail	
		TLI 6	1	120v Constant Power	2	L5-20 Flush	
			1	ETC NET	1	RJ45	
CSD1	18' Conector Strip						Left Feed
		DRA 81-86	6	20A Dimmed	6	24" Stage Pin Pigtail	
		TLI 7	1	120v Constant Power	2	L5-20 Flush	
			1	ETC NET	1	RJ45	
CSD2	18' Conector Strip	DRA 87-96					Right Feed
		TLI 8	10	20A Dimmed	10	24" Stage Pin Pigtail	

Figure 46 - Sample raceway schedule.

RACEWAY SCHEDULES

If our design has a series of raceways, then it's a good idea to include a raceway schedule in addition to breaker panel and dimmer panel schedules. Since these devices are rarely used by commercial electricians, there is no common way of laying out a schedule for them. The best way to go about it is to make sure you have enough information for an electrician to easily identify the location of the raceway, its size, the number and types of connectors it should have, and any helpful notes such as which side of the raceway the power should feed.

DETAIL DRAWINGS

If there is any question that the electricians or installers may not completely understand any part of the lighting system, it is a good idea to include detail drawings to help illustrate that portion of the system. For example, most commercial electricians have never seen a theatrical lighting system with a raceway and schedule 40 pipe. Therefore, it's always a good idea to include a sample detail drawing illustrating how the raceway and pipe should be rigged.

Other examples that might require detail drawings are catwalks, front of house control booths, or dimmer rack details. Often times it is helpful to show several different perspectives of a detail drawing. One way to do this is to lay out multiple view ports on one page and show a different perspective in each view port as shown in the sample below.

Each of the drawings should have a complete title block with the name of the project, the scale of the drawing, a drawing number, a revision number, and any other pertinent information such as our contact information. The name of the project should be the most prominent feature of the title block and it is most likely the name of the church for which the lighting design was created. The drawing number often has a letter designation followed by a sequential number for each page of the documentation. The letter should be a logical abbreviation for the type of drawing, e.g., "LE" for lighting and electrical or "AV" for audio/visual. The revision number is very important for keeping track of changes along the way and also to make sure that everyone is working from the latest drawings that have been issued. It's also a good idea to include a logo of our design firm along with the contact information so that in case any of the trades have any questions they know how to contact us. It's also more professional looking and it could lead to more business in the future.

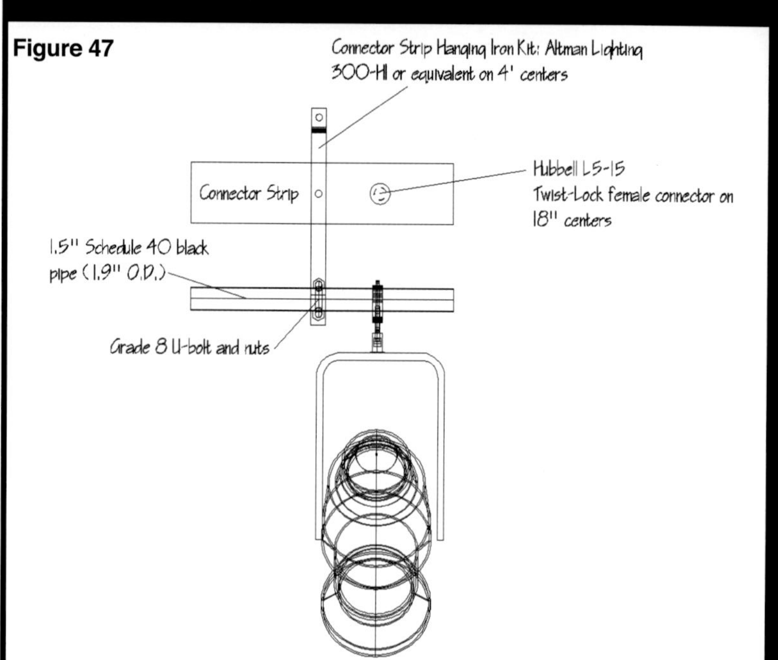

Figure 47 – Sample rigging detail showing raceway, rigging hardware, and raceway.

The assembled drawings should be printed and distributed as needed. Most every metropolitan area has several printers who can deal with architectural-sized print jobs. Many of them specialize in serving the architectural community and others, like FedEx-Kinkos, deal with a variety of customers. Care should be taken to insure that the prints are to scale. Blueprint shops are used to dealing with scale drawings but others are not. The ones who can best insure that the drawings will be to scale usually have an FTP site to upload DWG or DXF drawings. Better still are the ones who allow us to download a printer driver for their printer so that we can plot our drawings to a file from which they can print. Most of these shops also have technicians who can help us navigate their system or who will accept a file via e-mail rather than having to upload it to an FTP site.

SUMMARY

Delivering the final drawings is a milestone in the design process; it's not the end of the project, by any means, and chances are there will be many revisions before the project is completed. But being able to deliver a set of drawings is an accomplishment for which we should be pleased.

If we can start from the McCandless method and adapt it to our needs and create a finished lighting plot with the proper documentation, then we are well on our way to understanding the lighting design process. The information contained in this text is simply a starting point or a jumping off point, whether we want to make lighting design a career or whether we just want to know how best to design a lighting system for our own church. There is much to know and the best way to learn is by doing. Armed with the knowledge of the fundamentals, we should be confident that we can deal with just about any lighting situation with which we are confronted.

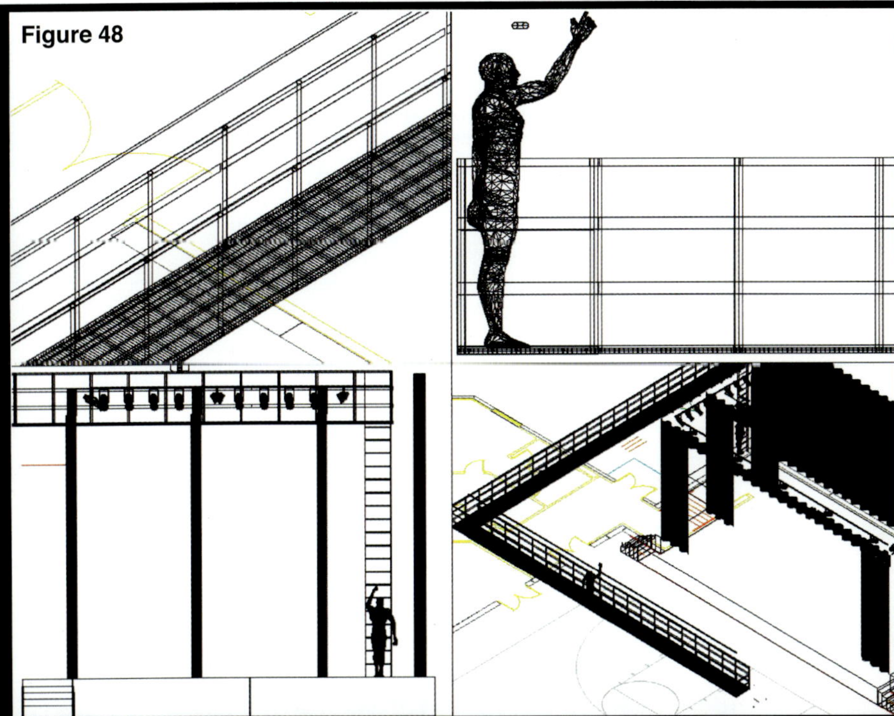

Figure 48 - Sample catwalk detail with several different perspectives.

Concepts:

- Photo-realistic renderings can aid in communicating the visualization of the final result of a new lighting design.
- Riser diagrams aid in the integration of various parts of a lighting system. They typically illustrate the wiring of low-voltage and high voltage (over 50 volts) systems.
- Various schedules can be created to assist in the execution of each task in the installation of a lighting system.

Words to Know

- Rendering – a computer simulated image.
- Riser diagram – a schematic representation of the wiring in a system from the feeder cable up to but not including individual branch circuits.
- Equipment schedule – a list of equipment and some of their attributes.
- Electrical one-line diagram – a schematic representation of an electrical distribution system drawn with one line instead of showing each individual wire.
- Patch schedule – a schedule showing each dimmer and the assigned channel on the lighting console.

APPENDIX A: GLOSSARY

3-point lighting system – a lighting system in which the subject is lit from three directions by the key light, the fill light and the backlight.

4-point lighting system – a lighting system in which the subject is lit from four directions by one key light, two fill lights and one backlight.

acting area – a 10' by 10' area of a stage representing a section of the lighting plot. Each acting area is individually lit to give more control over the entire system.

additive color mixing – Color synthesis by the addition of two or more colors. Lighting uses additive color mixing.

analogous colors – Two or more colors which are similar in hue.

backlight – light that is projected from behind a subject. Backlighting is used to highlight the outline of a subject, especially the hair and shoulders, and it helps give more separation from the background.

beam angle – the angle formed by the two points on the beam profile of a fixture at which the intensity is 50% of the peak, and the fixture.

blending distribution – a beam profile that produces a uniform area of coverage when blended with a like fixture. Also known as a cosine distribution.

B-roll – a video term describing pre-recorded content used to feed a video projector.

candela – a unit of measure of luminous intensity. Also known as candlepower. The illuminance in lux or footcandles is the luminous intensity in candelas divided by the square of the throw distance in meters or feet.

candlepower – a unit of measure of luminous intensity. Also known as candelas. The illuminance in lux or footcandles is the luminous intensity in candelas divided by the square of the throw distance in meters or feet.

chiaroscuro – Italian for light/dark. The use of bold contrast between light and dark for dramatic emphasis.

cold spot – an area that is lower in illuminance than the surrounding area.

color symbolism – The representation of meaning or feeling by means of color.

complementary colors – Two colors which, when added together, make white light.

computer-aided design (CAD) – a software that facilitates electronic drafting used to draw designs.

cosine distribution – a beam profile that follows a cosine function. Also known as a blending distribution.

CTB – correct to blue; a term used for any filter that shifts the color temperature of a lamp towards the blue end of the spectrum. They are often used to match tungsten sources to daylight sources.

CTO – correct to orange; a term used for any filter that shifts the color temperature of a lamp towards the red end of the spectrum. They are often used to match daylight sources to tungsten sources.

daylight – a source with a color temperature that matches natural light (5600K). The term is often used to denote a fixture with a high color temperature, such as "daylight fixture."

de-rate – the practice of lowering a value to allow for real-world factors. In electrical systems, the current carrying capacity of conductors is de-rated to compensate for excessive heat.

devitrification – the process by which glass loses its crystalline structure and becomes opaque through repeated cycles of heating and cooling.

dichroic – an optical thin-film that separates light into two parts. A dichroic filter is an optical thin-film filter on a glass substrate.

diffuse light – Indirect, scattered light.

directional light – Highly directed, non-scattered light.

discharge lamp – a lamp which discharges an arc between two electrodes to give light. A discharge lamp has no filament. The color temperature of discharge lamps range from about 5600K to 6800K or higher.

elevation – in a lighting system, the vertical distance from the subject to the height of the light. The elevation is not the same as the trim height because it does not include the height of the stage and the height to the target.

ellipsoidal reflector spotlight (ERS) – a luminaire in which the reflector geometry is a revolved ellipse, has a focal plane and produces a hard-edged beam.

exposure value – A combination of shutter speed and aperture setting that determines the exposure to light in a picture.

field angle – the angle formed by the two points on the beam profile at which the intensity is 10% of the peak, and the fixture.

fill light – the secondary light source in a lighting system. Fill light is used to fill in the shadows created by the key light.

footcandle – a unit of measure of illuminance equal to one lumen per square foot in the English system.

front of house (FOH) – the area downstage of the proscenium or the stage including the seating area. The control booth from where the lighting is operated is often referred to as the front of house.

frost – a filter used to soften the edge of a beam of light. A light frost filter works well with fill light to fill in shadows.

f-stop – An exposure value on a camera that corresponds to a doubling or halving of the light reaching the sensor.

gradient density filter – A filter that gradually increases in density as it moves into the optical path. CYM color mixing uses gradient density filters to control the amount of color in the beam.

hot spot – an area that is higher in illuminance than the surrounding area.

hypotenuse – the longest side of a right triangle, which is also the side opposite the right angle (90 degree angle).

illuminance – a unit of measure of the density of light falling on a surface area. Illuminance is the luminous flux (lumens) divided by the area. If the area is measured in square meters then the value of illuminance is given in lux and if the area is measured in square feet then the value is given in footcandles.

illuminance meter – an instrument used to measure illuminance.

I-mag – short for image magnification, a term used for the projection of video in order to magnify the subject and bring it closer to an audience.

incandescent lamp – a lamp which works on the principle of incandescence, the process of heating an object, in this case a filament, until it glows and gives light. The color temperature of an incandescent lamp is 3200K.

inverse square law – a law defining the relationship between the illuminance (lux or footcandles), the luminous intensity (candelas) and the throw distance. The illuminance is equal to the luminous intensity divided by the square of the throw distance.

jewel lighting – a lighting method in which the subject is lit from at least four or more directions. The name is derived from the effect in which the subject is said to sparkle like a jewel.

key light – the strongest light or set of lights in a lighting system. In a 3-point lighting system the key light is usually projected at a 45 degree angle relative to the subject and 45 degrees above the horizontal.

LD Assistant – the trade name of a CAD, paperwork and visualization software package made by Design & Drafting.

Leko – an ellipsoidal spotlight named after Irving Levy and Edward F. Kook of Century Lighting. The Leko was developed in 1932 by Century Lighting for a Broadway show called "Dead End."

live video reinforcement – the use of video capture and projection used to enhance a live event.

lumen – a unit of measure of luminous flux.

lumen depreciation – the loss of light output over time due to de vitrification and bulb wall blackening.

luminous flux – the density of light produced by a light source. The unit of measure of luminous flux is lumens.

luminous intensity – the measure of the strength or intensity of light in a particular direction. The unit of measure of luminous intensity is the candela.

lux – a unit of measure of illuminance equal to one lumen per square meter in the metric system.

McCandless method – a method of stage lighting developed by Stanley McCandless that involves dividing the stage into acting areas, lighting each acting area from opposite angles from the front, blending the lights, lighting the background and creating special effects. Adding backlight to the McCandless method produces a 3-point lighting system.

metric – a standard of measurement.

minus green filter – a filter that shifts the color of a light away from green and towards magenta. They are often used to correct lights that appear greenish on camera.

mireds – Microreciprocal degrees. The inverse of the color temperature multiplied by 1,000,000.

mired shift – A measure of the amount of shift in color temperature provided by a particular color correction filter.

modeling – the use of light projected onto a subject at an angle in order to highlight and define the shape and form of an object.

photometric data – a set of data describing the performance of a luminaire. Photometric data usually includes information about the field and beam angles, luminous flux, luminance, and sometimes the illuminance.

primary color – The most basic colors from which other color are derived and which cannot be derived from other colors. The additive primary colors are red, blue and green.

Pythagorean Theorem – a formula describing the relationship between the three sides of a right triangle.

right triangle – a triangle in which one of the three angles is a right angle (90 degree angle).

secondary – Those colors which are derived from the addition of two primary colors. The additive secondary colors are cyan, yellow and magenta.

setback – in a lighting system, the distance from the subject to the vertical plane in which a light is rigged, or the horizontal distance from the subject to the light.

shutter cut – the act of controlling the beam of an ellipsoidal reflector spotlight with the shutters.

signal-to-noise – the ratio between the voltage of a video signal and the voltage of the background noise in the signal.

subtractive – Relating to the subtraction of two or more colors. Color filters use subtractive mixing.

tangent – a trigonometric function equal to the ratio of the side opposite the angle in question and the hypotenuse.

tertiary – Those colors which are derived from the addition of one primary and one secondary color. The additive tertiary colors are blue-cyan, cyan-green, green-yellow, orange, red-magenta, and indigo.

thin-film optical filter – A glass filter manufactured by the deposition of multiple layers of dielectric material. Dichroic filters and glass gobos are thin-film optical filters.

throw – the distance light travels from a luminaire to its target.

triad – A group of three colors that are equidistant from each other on the color wheel.

trim – the vertical distance from the floor to the rigging point in a lighting system.

tungsten – the type of metal from which a lamp filament is made. The term is often used interchangeably with "incandescent," as in "tungsten source."

Vectorscope – an instrument used by video engineers to gauge the chromaticity or color content of a video signal.

Vectorworks – the trade name of a CAD and paperwork software package made by Nemetschek.

WYSIWYG – the trade name of a CAD, paperwork and visualization software package made by Cast Software.

APPENDIX B: USEFUL FORMULAS

- Formula relating illuminance, luminous flux and the area of the beam: Illuminance (footcandles or lux) = luminous flux (lumens) ÷ area (square feet or square meters)

- Formula for calculating the number of fixtures needed to uniformly cover the width of the stage: Width of wash (feet) = [number of fixtures -1] x diameter of beam (feet)

- Illuminance (footcandles) = luminous intensity (candelas) ÷ [throw distance (feet)]^2

- Pythagorean Theorem as it relates to lighting: Throw distance^2 = setback^2 + elevation^2

- Formula for tangents: Tangent Ø = opposite side ÷ hypotenuse

- Mireds: M = 1,000,000 ÷ color temperature (K)

- Mired Shift: Mired Shift = [1,000,000 ÷ starting color temperature (K)] + [1,000,000 ÷ ending color temperature (K)]